MW00337218

DIGITAL COMMUNICATIONS PROFESSIONALS

PRACTICAL CAREER GUIDES

Series Editor: Kezia Endsley

DIGITAL COMMUNICATIONS PROFESSIONALS

A Practical Career Guide

KEZIA ENDSLEY

ROWMAN & LITTLEFIELD
Lanham • Boulder • New York • London

Published by Rowman & Littlefield
An imprint of The Rowman & Littlefield Publishing Group, Inc.
4501 Forbes Boulevard, Suite 200, Lanham, Maryland 20706
www.rowman.com

6 Tinworth Street, London, SE11 5AL, United Kingdom

British Library Cataloguing in Publication Information Available

Library of Congress Cataloging-in-Publication Data

Names: Endsley, Kezia, 1968– author.
Title: Digital communications professionals : a practical career guide / Kezia Endsley.
Description: Lanham : Rowman & Littlefield, [2021] | Series: Practical career guides | Includes bibliographical references. | Summary: "This book includes interviews with professionals in digital communications, a field that has proven to be a stable, lucrative, and growing profession"—Provided by publisher.
Identifiers: LCCN 2021003925 (print) | LCCN 2021003926 (ebook) | ISBN 9781538145180 (paperback ; permanent paper) | ISBN 9781538145197 (epub)
Subjects: LCSH: Digital communications—Vocational guidance. | Social Media—Vocational guidance. | Multimedia communications—Vocational guidance. | Web site development—Vocational guidance.
Classification: LCC TK5102.6 .E53 2021 (print) | LCC TK5102.6 (ebook) | DDC 384.3023—dc23
LC record available at https://lccn.loc.gov/2021003925
LC ebook record available at https://lccn.loc.gov/2021003926

♾™ The paper used in this publication meets the minimum requirements of American National Standard for Information Sciences—Permanence of Paper for Printed Library Materials, ANSI/NISO Z39.48-1992.

Contents

Introduction

So You Want a Career in Digital Communications

*W*elcome to a career in digital communications! If you are interested in finding out about careers under the digital communications umbrella, you've come to the right book. This book is an ideal start for understanding the various careers available to you. It discusses the different paths you can follow to ensure you have all the training, education, and experience needed to succeed in your career goals.

A career in digital communications can be creative and fulfilling. *valentinrussanov/E+/Getty Images*

There is a lot of good news about this field. Job outlook is good, and job satisfaction is high. It's a great career choice for anyone with a desire to make a living using their creativity and writing skills in a professional setting.

When considering any career, your goal should be to find your specific nexus of interest, passion, and job demand. Although it is important to consider job outlook and demand, educational requirements, and other such practical matters, remember that you'll be spending a large portion of your life at whatever career you choose, so you should also find something that you enjoy doing and are passionate about. Of course, it can make the road easier to walk if you choose something that's in demand and pays the bills as well.

A Career in Digital Communications

Many, many professional titles fall under the umbrella of digital communications. In this book, we've made an effort to break them into areas that differ enough and that all have a strong job outlook in the foreseeable future. This book covers the following job areas:

- Digital media/content creation specialists
- Digital advertising and marketing professionals
- Social media specialists
- SEO (search engine optimization) and web analytics specialists
- Podcasters

This book discusses these main areas and the day-to-day responsibilities of each.

So what exactly do professionals in digital communications do on the job, day in and day out? What kinds of skills and educational background do you need to succeed in this field? How much can you expect to make, and what are the pros and cons of each area? How do you determine if digital communications is a good fit for you and which area best fits your talents and interests? This book can help you answer these questions and more.

For each of these areas of digital communications, the book covers the pros and cons, the educational requirements, projected annual wages, personality traits that match, working conditions and expectations, and more. You'll even read some interviews from real digital communications professionals working in these various jobs. The goal is for you to learn enough about digital communications in all its iterations to give you a clear view as to which career path is a food fit. And, if you still have more questions, we will also point you to resources where you can learn even more.

The Job Market Today

The U.S. Bureau of Labor Statistics is part of the U.S. Department of Labor. Its *Occupational Outlook Handbook* (see www.bls.gov/ooh) tracks statistical information about thousands of careers in the United States. Because the digital communications field is so broad, diverse, and dynamic, it's best to look at several different occupations to get the best overall picture of the market. The *Occupational Outlook Handbook* includes the following forecasts for jobs similar to or fitting within the digital communications umbrella:

- Public relations specialists are expected to experience job growth of about 7 percent between 2019 and 2029, which is faster than the average job growth rate (which is about 1.4 percent).[1]
- Careers within advertising, promotions, and marketing are expected to enjoy a growth of about 6 percent in the next decade.[2]
- Careers within the marketing research umbrella are expected to grow 18 percent in the next decade.[3]
- Careers under the social media specialists umbrella are expected to grow around 10 percent in the next decade.[4]
- Careers in podcasting are also expected to grow about 10 percent in the next decade.[5]

Print publishing and the use of print materials continue to shrink as more and more information is presented visually on phones and computer screens. Conversely, companies are continuing to increase their digital presence, requiring digital communicators to help market and curate their content to users. Although employment of communications specialists in newspaper, periodical, book, and directory publishers is projected to decline significantly, job prospects are strong for those who specialize in *digital* communications in one format or another.[6]

The bottom line? Job prospects will be best if you keep up with the latest trends, technologies, and techniques. Chapter 1 covers lots more about the job prospects in these areas and breaks down the numbers in each area into more detail.

What Does This Book Cover?

The goal of this book is to cover every aspect of digital communications and explain how the various areas are different and how you can excel in them. Here's a breakdown of the chapters:

- Chapter 1 explains the different careers under the umbrella of digital communications that are covered in this book. You'll learn about what digital communication specialists mentioned in this introduction do in their day-to-day work, the different environments where you can find people working, some pros and cons about each, the average salaries of these jobs, and the outlook for digital communications in general.
- Chapter 2 explains the educational requirements of these different fields, from high school diplomas to bachelor's degrees and beyond. You will learn how to go about getting experience (in the form of internships, for example) in these various settings before you enter college, as well as during your college years.
- Chapter 3 explains every aspect of college and postsecondary schooling that you'll want to consider as you move forward. You will learn how to get the best education for the best deal. You will also learn a little about scholarships and financial aid and how the SAT and ACT tests work.
- Chapter 4 covers every aspect of the interviewing and résumé-writing processes, including creating a dynamic portfolio that conveys your unique creative style, writing a stellar résumé and cover letter, interviewing to your best potential, dressing for the part, communicating effectively, dealing with stress, and more.

If you want to get into this career because you like posting pictures and you think that's fun, that's fine, but it won't be enough to sustain a career. Writing and communication skills are critical. You don't have to be an English professor, but you do need to hone your ability to write well, in different ways.—Michelle B. Freed, social media communications consultant

---

Where Do You Start?

You can approach the digital communications field in a few different ways—you can come to the field from a creative perspective and focus on creative writing, you can focus on computer programming and development and come to the career from a more technical angle, or you can study marketing/advertising/public relations and come to the career from that angle. In any case, you will need to meld the creative and artistic with knowledge of technologies and communication as they change in our evolving digital world.

The good news is that you don't need to know the answers to these questions yet. To find the best fit for yourself in digital communications, you need to understand how these different career options are structured. That's where you'll start in chapter 1.

Your future awaits. *Delpixart/iStock/Getty Images*

LAUREN WRIGHTON, PODCAST MANAGER AND PRODUCER

Lauren Wrighton. *Courtesy of Lauren Wrighton*

Lauren Wrighton received her bachelor's degree in neurobiology from Purdue University. She has been working in the podcasting industry since 2016. While looking for a remote part-time job that complemented her family obligations, she became interested in podcasting.

Lauren works with podcasters to produce their shows. She helps them land and schedule their guests. She edits and schedules the episodes and handles all areas of promotion, such as social media promotions and blogs.

Can you explain how you ended up in the podcasting arena? What about it interested you?

First off, I loved to listen to podcasts. At the time, I was working part-time in fitness, and a friend and I started our own podcast. I taught myself how to edit and launch a show from YouTube videos. I noticed that the industry was booming and saw an opportunity to help other podcasters manage their shows.

What's a "typical" day in your job? What do you do, day to day?

I work about 20 hours a week. I talk to clients during the day, but I primarily work at night since I have three small children. During that time, I am editing the show, scheduling the guests, and working on blogs and social media promotions. I work about three hours at night each day.

The majority of it is independent work. I help podcasters find guests based on a topic they want to discuss, or I help them contact specific guests that they want to ask to the show. I write blogs for the podcasters' websites as a summary of the episodes.

I create graphics and clips of the shows as teasers that I put on social media. Or I might produce written quotes. I send this promotional material to guests so they can promote the show on their channels as well. There are a lot of writing skills that come into play with podcast management as well.

What is the best part of being in this field? Is it what you expected it would be?

The best thing is that it's a lot of fun, and it's growing so much. Now is an exciting time to be doing podcasting. I also like controlling my own workload and the freedom I have to make my own schedule and work when it's best for me. I have independence and freedom.

What's the greatest challenge the market faces at this time?

Podcasters have a lot of questions about how to monetize their shows. There is a lot to learn in this arena. DIY (do-it-yourself) is harder in this sense. Learning that piece of it is hard in addition to the other skills. If you can help your podcasters monetize, you are a step ahead of many people out there.

Being strategic is also important—it's a long-term strategy. It's fun to start, but to keep it going is harder. You need an end goal.

Do you think your education adequately prepared you for your current career path?

Well, literally speaking, no, because it's not related. But I have been able to take things that I learned through other jobs. It's soft skills over hard skills, skills such as being a quick learner, being able to start a project before all the information is in, being flexible in that way, and communication skills for sure. Just trying different things out, like you do in college, has really helped me. Talking with other people and trying new things were things I honed in college, and those skills help me a lot now.

Where do you see this field going in the future?

I believe this field is in a big boom. It's been around a long time, but it's taken on this new form. There are 90,000 new shows every month, especially with the COVID-19 pandemic. I imagine that the technical side of it will completely transform. It will become easier, and the barrier to entry will be smaller. Tools will be developed to make it easier, including being able to get statistics on a podcast's success and other important information.

What traits or skills make for a good digital communications professional?

You have to be a go-getter and take initiative. You also have to be detail oriented but also see the big picture. You have to be able to always remember who you talking to while you also manage the details. You have to see the goal and end product and know who your audience is. Good communication skills are important too.

What advice do you have for young people considering this career? How can a young person prepare for this career while in high school?

You can learn a lot through self-education, from YouTube and so on. Start by learning different technical areas of websites. Learn how businesses are using social media to promote their websites. Learn the principles of marketing—digital marketing and general.

Be sure to listen to podcasts that you like. Listen to all different types of podcasts, and you'll learn what works and what is good about different types of shows. Figure out the audience.

Check out the website called udemy.com, which is inexpensive. You can learn podcasting skills from there. Also, take marketing classes in college. Content, no matter what it's about, will ultimately need to be properly marketed.

If you're looking for work, one way to land clients as a podcast manager is through a freelancing site, such as upwork.com.

Any last thoughts?

If you are interested in radio, you could also be interested in podcasting. There is lots of crossover. Learn about radio communications, as it's another entry into podcasting.

Why Choose a Career in Digital Communications?

*Y*ou learned in the introduction that the digital communications fields are varied, strong, and growing. You learned that, to have the best prospects for success, you need to learn and keep up with technology as well as learn how to communicate effectively. You also were reminded that it's important to pursue a career that you enjoy, are good at, and are passionate about. You will spend a lot of your life working; it makes sense to find something you enjoy doing. Of course you want to make money and support yourself while doing it. If you love the idea of being creative for a living, you've come to the right book.

The field of digital communications involves many aspects of communicating online, including collaboration, planning, and design. *scyther5/iStock/Getty Images*

In this chapter, we break out the job areas that typically fall under the "digital communications" umbrella and cover the basics of each. After reading this chapter, you should have a good understanding of several of the areas within digital communications, and you can start to determine if one of them is a good fit for you. Let's start with discussing what these folks actually do on the job.

What Do Digital Communicators Do?

When you think of someone in the digital communications field, you may picture a lot of different scenarios. You may picture a person working over a laptop, creating websites and brochures; someone pushing out targeted social media content for their company; someone writing Hypertext Markup Language (HTML), Cascading Style Sheets (CSS), and other code to create attractive websites; someone running and interpreting web analytics data to determine who is visiting their website; or even someone recording and producing a podcast. Digital communicators do all these things and more.

In addition to the different programs and technologies they use, the work of a digital communicator varies greatly, depending on the field they work in, the purpose of their projects (to sell something, to evoke emotion, to convince, and so on), the media in which they work, and more. That's good news because it means there are a lot of choices and options in these fields. To maximize your career options, you need to make sure you continue to educate yourself about changes in the field. Chapters 2 and 3 cover the educational requirements in more detail.

Recall that this book breaks the digital communications field into the following jobs:

- Digital media/content creation specialists
- Digital advertising and marketing professionals
- Social media specialists
- SEO (search engine optimization) and web analysis specialists
- Podcasters

The next sections discuss each of these career areas in more detail.

WHAT QUALITIES DO YOU NEED TO
SUCCEED IN DIGITAL COMMUNICATIONS?

Regardless of whether you're leaning more toward social media, general content creation, digital advertising, web analysis, or some mix of all of these, there is a core list of important qualities that you'll need to have or at least sharpen throughout time. They are as follows:

- **Communication skills:** You need to work as part of a team, be able to convey your ideas articulately, and compromise when needed. This includes verbal and written communication.
- **Flexibility and adaptability:** You must be ready to change gears or give up on an idea that you really like and slaved over if it doesn't work for the company or your client. You always have to be prepared to adopt new practices, update your skill set and knowledge base, keep up with industry best practices, and stay current with the latest technologies and trends.
- **Analytical skills:** You must be able to perceive your work from a consumer or client point of view to ensure that the words convey the intended message.
- **Computer skills:** You very likely use computer programs or write programming code to do most of your work.
- **Creativity:** You must be able to think creatively to develop original ideas and help them come to life.
- **Concentration:** You must sit at a computer and write or create content for long periods.
- **Thick skin:** You must be able to respond well to criticism and feedback and learn not to take it personally, even when it's your personal vision that's being rejected.
- **Time management skills:** Workdays can be long, particularly when there are tight deadlines. You'll need to be able to manage your time effectively when a deadline approaches.[1]

Most of these skills can be refined and polished with experience, education, and hard work, so worry not if you don't feel like you are "there" yet. If it's what you want, perseverance is key.

Digital Media/Content Creation Specialists

The meaning of the job title "content creation specialist" can vary greatly depending on the field you work in and the company you work for. This title can refer to web designers/developers, brand managers, HTML code writers, marketing experts, and more.

Here are some of the typical things that digital content creation specialists are tasked with:

- Designing digital media campaigns aligned with business goals (alone or as part of a marketing team)
- Coordinating the creation of digital content (website, blogs, press releases, and podcasts)
- Managing end-to-end digital projects
- Helping to establish the company's web presence to promote brand awareness
- Maintaining a strong online company voice through social media
- Working with marketing, sales, and product development teams to ensure brand consistency
- Suggesting and implementing direct marketing methods to increase profitability
- Staying up to date with digital media developments[2]

If you work as a content creation specialist, you will likely be expected to work well in a team setting whereby you develop the ideas and campaigns in conjunction with others, all of whom work on different aspects.

PERSISTENCE IS TRAINABLE

When your goal is to enter a creative and competitive field, such as social media design, SEO, or digital communications of any kind, being persistent is important to your ultimate success. The good news is that persistence is a skill that you can teach yourself. So how do you become persistent?

- **Know your goals:** It's easier to keep moving if you can see where you're going.

- **Keep your goals reachable:** How do you eat an elephant? One bite at a time. Don't frighten yourself with large, distant goals. Instead, focus on the next thing you need to do—turn an assignment in on time, critique a website, create a logo, and so on.
- **Know your priorities:** You already know what your priorities are. Get your schoolwork done. Get your work work done. Hang with your friends. Call your mom. And write content (not necessarily in that order).
- **Make digital communications a priority:** Take time to study the online communication all around you and be sure to carve out time in your schedule to work on your own ideas.
- **Use positive self-talk:** Don't let your inner voice give you a hard time. We all have a nasty little inner voice that makes us doubt ourselves. Counter that voice by purposely talking to yourself in a supportive and positive way (no, not out loud). Tell yourself, "I'm just going to do this now."
- **Get in the habit of getting in the habit:** Pick a thing and do it. Then pick another thing and do that. Repeat.
- **Notice when you finish:** Pay attention to those special times when you complete a project. Feel proud of yourself. See how nice that is? Noticing how good it feels to finish something helps you be persistent in the future. Creating something from nothing takes patience at every stage. Patience doesn't mean sitting around waiting for opportunities to come to you. Patience means accepting that things take time and that fretting and stressing about it doesn't make things happen any sooner. Patience means accepting that if one opportunity doesn't work out, there is always another one.
- **Have faith in yourself and your work:** Perhaps the most important thing that you'll need is to have faith in yourself. Some people seem to be born confident, talented, or both. Others need to develop it over the course of a lifetime. Faith in yourself doesn't mean arrogance or the assumption that you have nothing new or different to learn. It means an internal confidence in your ability to learn, to imagine, and to create that will carry you during difficult times. It means learning to recognize what is good in your work without relying only on the opinions of others. It also means being confident enough in your abilities to recognize when an idea is not working so that you can either fix it or set it aside and move on to something else.

Digital Advertising and Marketing Professionals

The digital advertising or marketing specialist will often be tasked with many of the roles that content creation specialists take on. Because the line between standard/informational content and marketing content has blurred on the internet so much, these titles are often one and the same. Of course, this can vary greatly, depending on the field in which you work.

Digital advertisers and marketing professionals focus on "selling the sizzle," as they say. Their role essentially involves designing, creating, and delivering effective online marketing programs that support the company's services and products. The goal may be to increase brand awareness or create a brand image, to identify a target market, to promote company products or services, to drive prospects to conversions (sales), or a combination of all these.

You may choose to specialize in certain areas, such as SEO, paid search (PPC, or *pay-per-click*), display media, social media, or shopping feeds. Or you can have more general digital marketing expertise and still be referred to as a digital marketing specialist.

Key skills you'll need to be a digital marketing specialist include the following:

- Knowing marketing principles in the key areas of SEO, social media, content marketing, e-mail marketing, and PPC
- Being creative and having good presentation skills
- Knowing how to plan, create, and implement a marketing strategy
- Understanding the key measurement tools available
- Developing a social presence and advocating brands effectively
- Staying current in marketing trends and news[3]

Social Media Specialists

Social media specialists communicate with the public through platforms that allow users to create and share content online. They run their company social media accounts, working to build the brand's reputation and ensure that it's consistent and positive.

They post content—such as images, text, and videos—to garner interest in a topic that relates to the company or its brand. In addition, social media specialists follow conversations and interact with the public online. These workers sometimes collaborate with others to promote their employer's cause. For example, they might work on a team with marketing consultants to publicize an event.

To track the effectiveness of their communication strategies, social media specialists will also set goals and then measure success against those goals.[4]

Web Analytics Specialists

Web analytics specialists, also known as web analysts or sometimes SEO specialists, determine the costs, benefits, drawbacks, and effectiveness of websites. In other words, they determine how well a site is doing what it set out to do by measuring the "traffic" (the visitors) that comes to it.

The web analytics specialist needs to be current on all the key measurement tools available and must be installing and using the latest tools as they constantly evolve. But that's not all they do. Because web analytics solutions (such as Google Analytics) more or less run unmanned once they're installed, the majority of their job isn't about collecting data but rather about *interpreting* it.

On a daily, weekly, monthly, quarterly, or annual basis, they generate and review reports that contain information about visitor demographics and behavior. They will likely present these reports to company stakeholders, such as CEOs, web designers, and marketing professionals.

For example, you could be tasked with determining how many people visited your website, where those people live, how long they stayed, what and how many web pages they viewed, where on the website they clicked, and what search terms they used to find your website in the first place.[5] This information is important to your employer/client because they can use it to improve the website so that the following occurs:

- Visitors stay longer.
- Visitors find what they are looking for easily.
- Visitors are encouraged to purchase something (if that's a feature of the site).

- Visitors leave the site with a favorable impression of the company.
- Information about visitors can be collected (with their permission, of course) so that the company can more effectively create marketing campaigns.

Web analysis is not typically an entry-level position. As a web analyst, you'll need to be able to interpret web traffic data, visualize data appropriately, understand the dynamics behind a website, integrate market research, and use and understand web analytics tools and interpret the data you get from them. A background or degree in marketing is a good place to start.

Podcast Producer

Although podcasting itself has been around for more than 15 years, the role of the podcast producer as a career path is relatively new. It's still at an early enough stage that many people dive into this career by self-educating and trial and error. This book focuses on the podcast producer as a career path rather than as simply a stand-alone podcaster who may or may not make a living off a podcast.

So what do podcast producers do? At the least, they have a hand in content creation and production. They might help develop shows and episode content, write scripts and stories, participate in brainstorming sessions, and help find and hire guests to speak on the podcast. They are also typically involved in the audio recording and editing process. You should know how to record audio that sounds good, how to put a project together and edit it using audio software, how to write narration (if necessary), add music, mix and master, and whatever else the production process requires. You may also be tasked with advertising and marketing the podcast so that your intended audience can find it.

Skills needed to be successful are as follows:

- **Ability to work well with others:** You should be able to work with— and possibly manage—producers, writers, audio engineers, editors, freelancers, guests, and so on.
- **Technical skills:** You will use audio and music software and will have to learn or teach yourself new programs as well as troubleshoot when you run into technical glitches.
- **Ability to work under deadlines:** You can get stuff done and shipped on schedule (time management skills).

- **Problem-solving skills:** There's going to be stuff they don't know and stuff you don't know, so you should be able and willing to figure it out.
- **Leadership skills:** You have opinions and taste and are comfortable with setting goals and identifying how you'll measure success.[6]

The Pros and Cons of the Digital Communications Field

Keep in mind that in a small company or start-up, the digital communicator may be responsible for some combination of all the roles described in the previous sections. They aren't always separate jobs. That means you'll need some technical know-how, some marketing savvy, great communications skills, and a good mix of people and technical skills. Chapter 2 covers the educational expectations in full.

As with any career, one in digital communications has upsides and downsides. But also true is that one person's "pro" is another person's "con." If you love working in teams and collaborating with others, then this could well be the right job for you. But if you prefer to work solo, it's probably going to be frustrating for you at times. Equally, if you like the rush of a hurried deadline and ever-changing specifications and due dates and don't mind working long hours at times, then you will get a charge out of digital communications.

LEARNING BY "SEEING"

Although it's one thing to *read* about the pros and cons of a particular career, the best way to really get a feel for what a typical day is like on the job and learn about the challenges and rewards is to talk to someone who is working in the profession. It's also a good idea to arrange to *job shadow* with a professional in the field in whichever capacity you find most interesting to you. This means accompanying someone to work and observing the tasks they perform, the work culture, the environment, the hours, and the intensity of the work. Talk with people you know who work in the business. You can also learn a lot by reading the interviews with actual professionals that you find sprinkled throughout this book.

Although each profession within digital communications is different, there are some generalizations that can be made when it comes to what is most challenging about the field and most gratifying.

> With digital offerings, I really enjoy connecting with people on a level that's not possible in a monthly print magazine. You can reach people and share a story on a mass scale. These stories feel personal once you've spent time researching and writing them. You get invested, so it's especially cool to reach people all over the country and get so much immediate feedback. That is so cool, gratifying, and humbling. It's a concentrated dose of print, totally sped up.—Michael Rubino, editor in chief, *Indianapolis Monthly*

Here are some general pros:

- The work tends to be creative and challenging.
- You'll get paid to spend time on your favorite platforms.
- You also can potentially get real-time feedback about how you're doing.
- In this competitive field, you will have colleagues who share your passion and from whom you can learn.
- Your work has the potential to go viral or have a positive impact.
- It is a constantly evolving field with new trends and innovations and an endless opportunity for learning.
- There's a vast degree of variety in work environments, from large corporations to start-ups to freelance work from anywhere.
- The kind of degree you need is flexible—you can choose one of several paths to a career in digital communications.

Here are some general cons:

- The working hours can be long and irregular. You can expect at times to work early and late hours and also on weekends to meet a pressing deadline or deal with any number of unpredictable issues or situations that may arise.

- Because of the high level of collaboration, a writer or developer—or anyone on the team—can expect to have to surrender an idea or even a whole design that they feel attached to. You have to be flexible and think as a team rather than as an individual creator.
- It is a high-pressure field that requires an ability to manage stress well and to multitask. You need a thick skin to be able to handle criticism and feedback.
- It is a competitive field. Breaking in and advancing to the next level can take a lot of time, hard work, creativity, and patience.
- You have to constantly evolve to keep your performance up and continue to compete.

Collaborating with other smart and creative people who you respect can be one of the great joys of working in digital communications. *adimguzhva/iStock/Getty Images*

The good news is that you can control some of these factors. You can eliminate or mitigate many of these drawbacks by carefully choosing the environment you work in. Let's talk more about the job market next.

How Healthy Is the Job Market?

Recall in the introduction that you learned about the Bureau of Labor Statistics, which is part of the U.S. Department of Labor (see www.bls.gov). It tracks statistical information about thousands of careers in the United States. Data about careers in digital communications differ greatly depending on the area of focus/approach. Let's look at them each separately.

DIGITAL MEDIA/CONTENT CREATION SPECIALISTS

- **Education:** Varies from an associate degree in web design, marketing, public relations, or related field to a bachelor's degree in computer science or programming.
- **2020 median income:** $73,760.
- **Job outlook 2019–2029:** 8 percent (much faster than average).
- **Work environment:** In the computer systems design and related services industry. Some people are self-employed, and still others work in industries including publishing, management consulting, and advertising.[7]

DIGITAL ADVERTISING AND MARKETING PROFESSIONALS

- **Education:** Bachelor's degree in marketing, advertising, communications, or a related field.
- **2020 median income:** $135,900 at the manager level.
- **Job outlook 2019–2029:** 6 percent (faster than average).
- **Work environment:** Work in advertising, public relations, and related services or be freelance/self-employed.[8]

SOCIAL MEDIA SPECIALISTS

- **Education:** Bachelor's degree in public relations, marketing, communications, business, or a related field.
- **2020 median income:** $56,700.
- **Job outlook 2019–2029:** 6 percent (faster than average).
- **Work environment:** In the computer systems design and related services industry. Some people are self-employed, and still others work in industries including publishing, management consulting, and advertising.[9]

WEB ANALYTICS SPECIALISTS/SEO

- **Education:** Bachelor's or master's degree in marketing, communications, business, or an information technology–related field.
- **2020 median income:** $48,590.
- **Job outlook 2019–2029:** 7 to 10 percent (faster than average).
- **Work environment:** Many of these workers are employed in specialized design services, publishing, or advertising, public relations, and related services industries.[10]

PODCASTERS

- **Education:** College degree not required but preferred. A background in marketing and technical knowledge is helpful.
- **2020 median income:** $25,000 to $75,000.
- **Job outlook 2019–2029:** 4 percent (average).
- **Work environment:** Most podcasters set up recording studios in their homes, which allows for greater flexibility in their working hours. Since podcast episodes are created and saved individually, podcasters can record several episodes in one day and release them as needed. Other podcasters, especially those who comment on current events and culture, record episodes daily.[11]

WHAT IS A MEDIAN INCOME?

Throughout your job search, you might hear the term "median income" being used. What does it mean? Some people believe it's the same thing as "average income," but that's not correct. While median income and average income might sometimes be similar, they are calculated in different ways.

The true definition of median income is the income at which half the workers earn more than that income and the other half of workers earn less. If this is complicated, think of it this way. Suppose there are five employees in a company, each with varying skills and experience. Here are their salaries:

- $42,500
- $48,250
- $51,600
- $63,120
- $86,325

What is the median income? In this case, the median income is $51,600 because of the five total positions listed, it is in the middle. Two salaries are higher than $51,600, and two are lower.

The "average income" is simply the total of all salaries divided by the number of total jobs. In this case, the average income is $58,359.

Why does this matter? The median income is a more accurate way to measure the various incomes in a set because it's less likely to be influenced by extremely high or low numbers in the total group of salaries. For example, in our example of five incomes, the highest income ($86,325) is much higher than the other incomes, and therefore it makes the average income ($58,359) well higher than most incomes in the group. Therefore, if you base your income expectations on the *average*, you'll likely be disappointed to eventually learn that most incomes are below it.

But if you look at median income, you'll always know that half the people are above it and half are below it. That way, depending on your level of experience and training, you'll have a better estimate of where you'll end up on the salary spectrum.

ERIK DAFFORN, SEO ANALYTICS CONSULTANT

Erik Dafforn. *Courtesy of Erik Dafforn*

Erik Dafforn received his bachelor's degree in English from Wabash College. He currently works as an SEO and analytics consultant. This means he helps clients build and maintain websites that people can find through search engines, and he helps companies understand all the traffic coming to their sites.

After working for an online marketing company for about 15 years, he started his own company about six years ago, and he's a one-person organization. He enjoys the freedom that this offers because delegating work has always been difficult for him. In his current role, he does all the work, and he gets either all the credit or all the blame for a project. He's okay with that.

Can you explain how you ended up in this field? What about it interested you? Is it what you expected it would be?

I landed in the internet marketing industry by accident. With an English degree, I started out in book publishing. After a few publishing jobs, I was working as a part-time contractor with an internet marketing company writing web page content, analysis documents, and press releases. I was intrigued by what the SEO team was doing because it seemed very mysterious but also very cool. This was before Google had a significant presence in the industry, so the engines we really focused on were AltaVista, Yahoo!, HotBot, Lycos, and other engines a lot of people don't remember.

I learned SEO from people who had been around at its very beginning. There were no published rules or guidelines—much like the entire internet was at that time. Today, there is a vast body of work out there about how to make your site perform well for search engines, and I was able to take part in writing some of that.

What's a "typical" day in your job?

In any given day, I do a variety of things, including the following:

- Build traffic reports or presentations for clients that show an analysis of their web traffic numbers and other usage statistics (online sales, time spent on-site, and so on).
- Make recommendations about how clients should change or build their websites. This includes explaining why I've made those recommendations and predicting what the results of those changes or actions will be.
- Use some of my tools to perform research into user behavior. This might be a key word research tool, which describes how people use search engines to find information. It might also be a user-experience (UX) tool, which shows how people interact with web pages—where they click, how far they scroll down the page, and so on.
- Meet with other teams or workers that work on the same projects I do. That might be the marketing team, programmers, or supervisors for a particular website.

Because I'm self-employed, I also do a lot of things that aren't directly in the cross-hairs of my discipline:

- Build and send invoices and contracts to clients
- Prepare sales pitches and presentations

What's the greatest challenge the market faces at this time? What are your greatest challenges day in and day out?

As an external consultant (someone who doesn't work full-time for any particular company), I face several challenges, and they all revolve around consistently being able to prove that I'm worth the money I charge to clients.

Many companies want to bring all their marketing resources "in house," which means they want to minimize the number of external contractors they use. Being an external contractor, it's up to me to show them that keeping me is a good deal for them. So it's not enough to simply help them when they have a problem; instead, I often need to identify their problems before they do and present a solution.

There is always a lot of new technology to keep track of. I get to see the most current techniques in web development, and it's my job to make sure those techniques still enable Google, for example, to properly interpret the content. So I spend a lot of time looking at code, crawling through a site like Google does, and making educated guesses about how a site redesign or code changes will affect a client's marketing numbers.

What's the best part of being in this field?

I really enjoy the clients that I work with. I enjoy helping them succeed and watching their businesses grow. I get to learn more about the industries that my clients are in, such as higher education, construction, property management, retail, and tourism.

I enjoy spending time with really smart people, and my clients are just that. They come from different backgrounds and different countries, but the common thread among them is their desire to do good work and succeed at their jobs.

What's the most challenging part of being in this field?

Search engines like Google are constantly innovating and modifying their code with the goal of ensuring that their users have a good experience on the site. This is important, but it can be hard to keep track of all the different features they offer and to know which ones are important and worth my clients' time. When my clients ask about a particular feature or search engine recommendation, I need to make sure I've not only heard about it but that I have an opinion on it before they ask. Keeping up with all the documentation can be a challenge.

Do you think your education adequately prepared you for your current job?

I do. Even though I was an English major, the foundation of my education consisted of doing research, building an argument or position, then using a narrative (either written or a spoken presentation) to describe and defend that claim. Today, much of what I do uses that same approach.

Where do you see this field going in the future?

People will always use technology to search for information, ask questions, and make transactions. The challenge will be to keep up with the different ways they do those things. Twenty years ago, this involved sitting at a large computer and typing search queries over and over until you found results that helped you. Today, people can buy things directly from a phone or ask a question to their smart speaker. Making sure your content is formatted for all these various methods of interaction—and that you can measure that interaction—will always be essential skills.

What traits or skills make for a good SEO/marketing manager?

I think the best SEO and marketing managers understand that while SEO is important, it's only one piece in a larger puzzle. This is a lesson that a lot of SEO workers have learned over time. If you build a website focused only on ensuring people *arrive* at the site, chances are the site won't contain a very fulfilling user experience once the visitors arrive.

Therefore, you need to build a site that attracts users but one that presents a very intuitive interface, easy access to information, and a pathway for the user to take the steps that are logical for her to complete her journey. This means using technology to ensure a fast-loading site, using design features that ensure the user finds the site appealing, and integrating user-experience (UX) features that make it easy and rewarding for the user to stick around on the site for a while.

And finally, you need to be able to measure your results accurately. It's not enough to say that 1,000 people visited your site. Which visitors were more engaged with the content? Were site visitors on a phone more valuable than those on a desktop machine? Which methods of drawing in visitors were the most effective, and which could be dropped?

What advice do you have for young people considering this career?

I think SEO and web marketing in general are good careers to consider because they touch so many other career types: web development, programming, brand management, e-commerce, advertising, and general marketing. You'll interact with smart people with a variety of skills, and you'll come away with a really broad understanding of how electronic communication plays out.

How can a young person prepare for this career while in high school?

Build a website. (Make sure the site is an extension of your own passions or hobbies, or else you won't enjoy it!) Install analytics and watch your traffic closely. How are visitors finding you? What can you do to increase your traffic or improve the user experience? And how can you prove, through data, that your changes resulted in better numbers? Those are all essential characteristics of a web marketer, and performing experiments in traffic generation—and being able to document and present them—will help you create an excellent portfolio.

Would I Succeed in Digital Communications?

This is a tough question to answer because really the answer can come only from you. But don't despair: there are plenty of resources both online and elsewhere that can help you find the answer by guiding you through the types of questions and considerations that will bring you to your conclusion.

Of course, no job is going to match your personality or fit your every desire, especially when you are just starting out. There are, however, some aspects to a job that may be so unappealing or simply mismatched that you may decide to opt for something else, or, equally, you may be so drawn to a feature of a job that any downsides are not that important.

> The digital world has enabled me to have this independent career that I could not have envisioned as a young person. What I continue to like about it is that I get to try out new technologies—hardware, software, platforms, and ways of working. I like digital tools that help you work smarter. When I am on my smartphone, I am being productive. I am a "work smarter, not harder" person, and I think technologies can help you do that now more than ever.—Lisa A. Bucki, author, trainer, and content expert

Having excellent communication skills and a passion for online communications in all its forms is particularly important in this field, of course. But there are other factors to keep in mind as well. One way to see if you may be cut out for this career is to ask yourself the following questions:

- *Am I a creative person who is also able to let an idea I may love go because others disagree or it just isn't possible?*
  Any creative person feels attached to his or her ideas. When you are working alone on your own vision, you have full control over what the end result will be. It doesn't work that way when you work creatively with a team and when you have a client who has a different vision and the ultimate say in how things look.
- *Am I able to follow directions even if I don't agree? Am I able to understand instructions quickly?*

Working in a team can be a fulfilling and inspiring experience, and this field does provide that for the most part. However, it does require being comfortable with others making final decisions and understanding quickly what you are tasked with doing.

- *Can I be creative under tight deadlines?*
Working under tight deadlines can be exhilarating, but it can also cause you to experience moments of "idea freeze." Can you work through those creative morasses? Are you willing to work some long hours and weekends when needed?

- *When something goes wrong, can I think quickly on my feet to find a solution? Do I have the leadership skills to direct others to solve problems?*
Because this is a fast-paced industry where everything can change at any time, being flexible and staying calm under pressure is paramount. Equally important is being able to provide solutions or suggestions when something goes awry.

- *Can I consistently deal with people in a professional, friendly way?*
Communication is a key skill to have in any profession, especially here, because it's important to convey clearly and concisely what your expectations as visions are.

If the answer to any of these questions is an adamant no, you might want to consider a different path. Remember that learning what you *don't* like can be just as important as figuring out what you do like to do.

Are you ready for a creative and rewarding career in digital communications? *meta-morworks/iStock/Getty Images*

If you pursue a career that fundamentally conflicts with the person you are, you won't be good at it, and you won't be happy. Don't make that mistake. Need help in determining your key personality factors? Take a career-counseling questionnaire to find out more. You can find many online or ask your school guidance counselor for reputable sources.

Summary

In this chapter, you learned a lot about the different types of careers that exist under the general "digital communications" umbrella. You've learned about what social media specialists do in comparison to content creation specialists, for example. You also learned about some pros and cons of this field, the median salaries of these jobs, and the outlook in the future for various aspects of digital communications. You may have even contemplated some questions about whether your personal likes and preferences meld well with this career. Are you starting to get excited about the idea of working in digital communications? If not, that's okay, as there's still time.

In chapter 2, we'll dive into forming a plan for your future. We cover everything there is to know about educational requirements, certifications, internship opportunities, and more for each of these areas of digital communications. You'll learn about finding summer jobs and learn how to start building a portfolio that has your own unique sensibility as well. The goal is for you to set yourself apart from—and above—the rest.

2

Forming a Career Plan

*I*t's not easy to choose a career, yet it's one of the most important decisions you will make in your life. There are simply so many options available, and it is easy to feel overwhelmed. Especially if you have many passions and interests, it can be hard to narrow your options down. That you are reading this book means you have decided to investigate a career in digital communications, which means you have already discovered a passion for communication, technology, and ongoing learning. But even within this industry, there are many choices, including what role you want to pursue, what work environment you desire, and what type of work schedule best fits your lifestyle.

Now that you have some idea about the different career opportunities within the digital communications umbrella, it's time to formulate a career plan. If you are organized, this can be a helpful and energizing process. If you're not a naturally organized person or perhaps the idea of looking ahead and building a plan to adulthood scares you, you are not alone. That's what this chapter is for.

After we talk about ways to develop a career plan (there is more than one way to do this), the chapter dives into the various educational requirements. Finally, we will look at how you can gain experience through school activities, such as a high school yearbook, a Twitter account, a newspaper, job shadowing, volunteering, part-time jobs, and more. Yes, experience will look good on your résumé, and in some cases it's even required. But even more important, getting out there and working in digital communications in various settings is the best way to determine if it's really something that you enjoy. When you find a career that you truly enjoy and have a passion for, it will rarely feel like work at all.

If you still aren't sure if the digital communications field is right for you, try a self-assessment questionnaire or a career aptitude test. There are many good ones on the web. As an example, the career-resource website monster.com includes its favorite free self-assessment tools at www.monster.com/career-advice

/article/best-free-career-assessment-tools. The Princeton Review also has a very good aptitude test geared toward high schoolers at www.princetonreview.com /quiz/career-quiz.

YOUR PASSIONS, ABILITIES, AND INTERESTS: IN JOB FORM

Think about how you've done at school and how things have worked out at any temporary or part-time job you've had so far. What are you really good at in your opinion? And what have other people told you you're good at? What are you not very good at right now but would like to become better at? What are you not very good at and you're okay with not getting better at?

Now forget about work for a minute. In fact, forget about needing to ever have a job again. You won the lottery—congratulations. Now answer these questions: What are your favorite three ways of spending your time? For each one of those things, can you describe why you think you in particular are attracted to it? If you could get up tomorrow and do anything you wanted all day long, what would it be? These questions can be fun but can also lead you to your true passions. The next step is to find the job that sparks your passions.

Your ultimate goal should be to match your personal interests/goals with your preparation plan for college/careers. Practice articulating your plans and goals to others. Once you feel comfortable speaking about your aspirations, that means you have a good grasp of your goals and can develop a clear plan to reach them.

Planning the Plan

The following are questions that are helpful to think about deeply when planning your career path:

- Think about your interests outside of the work context. How do you like to spend your free time? What inspires you? What kind of people do you like to surround yourself with, and how do you best learn? What do you really love doing?

- Brainstorm a list of the various career choices within the digital communications umbrella that you are interested in pursuing. Organize the list in the order of which careers you find most appealing and then list what it is about each that attracts you. This can be anything from work environment to geographical location to the type of communications to the specific role you desire.
- Research information on each job on your career choices list. You can find job descriptions, salary indications, career outlook, salary, and educational requirements information online, for example.
- Consider your personality traits. How do you respond to stress and pressure? Do you consider yourself a strong communicator? Do you work well in teams or prefer to work independently? Do you consider yourself creative? How do you respond to criticism? All of these are important to keep in mind to ensure you choose a career path that makes you happy and in which you can thrive.
- Although a career choice is obviously a huge factor in your future, it's important to consider what other factors feature in your vision of your ideal life. Think about how your career will fit in with the rest of your life, including whether you want to live in a big city or a small town, how much flexibility you want in your schedule, how much autonomy you want in your work, and what your ultimate career goal is.
- While there are lucrative careers in the digital communications field, many job opportunities that offer experience to newcomers and recent graduates can come with relatively low salaries. What are your pay expectations now and in the future?

Posing these questions to yourself, thinking about them deeply, and answering them honestly will help make your career goals clearer and guide you in knowing which steps you will need to take to get there.

You are on a fact-finding mission of sorts. A career fact-finding plan, no matter what the field, should include these main steps:

- Find out about educational requirements and schooling expectations. Will you be able to meet any rigorous requirements? This chapter will help you understand the educational paths.
- Seek out opportunities to volunteer or shadow someone doing the job. This will enable you to experience in person what the atmosphere is like,

what a typical workday entails, how coworkers interact with each other and with management, and how well you can see yourself thriving in that role and work culture. Use your critical thinking skills to ask questions and consider whether this is the right environment for you.

- Look into student aid, grants, scholarships, and other ways you can get help to pay for schooling.
- Build a timetable for taking requirement exams such as the SAT and ACT, applying to schools, visiting schools, and making your decision. You should write down all the important deadlines and have them ready when you need them.
- Continue to look for employment that matters during your college years—internships and work experiences that help you build hands-on experience and knowledge about your actual career.
- Talk with professionals working in the job you are considering and ask them what they enjoy about their work, what they find the most challenging, and what path they followed to get there.
- Find a mentor in the field who is interested in helping you. This person can be a great source of information, education, and connections. Don't expect a job (at least not at first); just build a relationship with someone who wants to pass along their wisdom and experience. Coffee meetings or even e-mails are a great way to start.

A mentor can help you in many ways. *martinedoucet/E+/ Getty Images*

Where to Go for Help

If you aren't sure where to start, your local library, school library, and guidance counselor office are great places to begin. Search your local or school library for resources about finding a career path and finding the right schooling that fits your needs and budget. Make an appointment with a counselor or e-mail one and ask about taking career interest questionnaires. With a little prodding, you'll be directed to lots of good information online and elsewhere. You can start your research with these five sites:

- The U.S. Department of Labor's Bureau of Labor Statistics Career Outlook site (www.bls.gov/careeroutlook/home.htm) doesn't just track job statistics, as you learned in chapter 1. There is an entire portion of this site dedicated to young adults looking to uncover their interests and match those interests with jobs currently in the market. There is a section called "Career Planning for High Schoolers" that you should check out. Information is updated based on career trends and jobs in demand, so you'll get practice information as well.
- The Mapping Your Future site at www.mappingyourfuture.org helps you determine a career path and then helps you map out a plan to reach those goals. It includes tips on preparing for college, paying for college, job hunting, résumé writing, and more.
- The Education Planner site at www.educationplanner.org has separate sections for students, parents, and counselors. It breaks down the task of planning your career goals into simple, easy-to-understand steps. You can find personality assessments, get tips for preparing for school, learn from some Q&As from counselors, download and use a planner worksheet, read about how to finance your education, and more.
- TeenLife at www.teenlife.com calls itself the "leading source for college preparation," and it includes lots of information about summer programs, gap-year programs, community service, and more. They believe that spending time out "in the world" outside of the classroom can help students do better in school, find a better fit in terms of career, and even interview better with colleges. This site contains lots of links to volunteer and summer programs.
- The educations.com site provides a career test designed to help you find the job of your dreams. Visit www.educations.com/career-test to take the test.

Use these sites as jumping-off points and don't be afraid to reach out to a real person, such as a guidance counselor or your favorite teacher, if you're feeling overwhelmed.

The process of deciding on and planning a career path is daunting. In many ways, the range of choices of careers available today is a wonderful thing. It allows us to refine our career goals and customize them to our own lives and personalities. In other ways, though, too much choice can be extremely daunting and requires a lot of soul-searching to navigate clearly.

Tip: Young adults with disabilities can face additional challenges when planning a career path. DO-IT (Disabilities, Opportunities, Internetworking, and Technology) is an organization dedicated to promoting career and education inclusion for everyone. Its website (www.washington.edu/doit) contains a wealth of information and tools to help all young people plan a career path, including self-assessment tests and career exploration questionnaires.

MICHELLE B. FREED, SOCIAL MEDIA COMMUNICATIONS CONSULTANT

Michelle B. Freed. *Courtesy of Michelle B. Freed*

Michelle B. Freed received her bachelor's degree in journalism from the University of Oklahoma with a public relations (PR) emphasis. Her initial focus was on PR and corporate communications. She has spent most of her career in nonprofit communications, currently running her communications consultant company called WoodFish.

At this time, she mainly focuses on social media, although she does enjoy working with teams determining the messages and helping with content writing and strategy.

Can you explain how you ended up in PR? What about it interested you?

At the time, I liked marketing and communications. My main goal in journalism is that I loved to write and was a very curious person. I loved learning about other people. I didn't really want to be a reporter per se. PR seemed like the best fit at the time.

I worked at a PR agency as well as many nonprofits. My job evolved into writing, which I enjoyed the best. I was a person of all trades—designing, producing, and writing. I created newsletters, nonprofit magazines, etcetera. Computers were crude at that time. I started learning about software as it became available. I taught myself because that was where the direction was going. I learned coding, design, and so on.

I didn't think about social media until many of my clients about 10 years ago began wanting help with it. The social media umbrella became something clients really wanted, so I added that to my tool kit. I'm largely self-taught in these areas.

I do online content, social media management, and messaging throughout all mediums (online, mailers, etc.). My career moved to digital world.

I am mostly self-taught. Social media evolves all the time. You have to be self-motivated and learn constantly. One way I learn is by partnering with digital marketing companies. The analytics and strategy people teach me a lot, and I do more of the creative part. They do more behind-the-scenes coding and analysis.

To be successful, you have to have a good base of communication skills and good knowledge of marketing and strategy. You have to constantly learn new things.

What's a "typical" day in your job? What do you do, day to day?

I am a freelancer running my own communications consultant company called WoodFish. I have several large companies I work with regularly, and they are often more structured as well as smaller companies with short-term projects that tend to be more intense for shorter periods of time. You have to adapt to client needs and expectations.

There really is no typical day, although I do structure my week somewhat. Mondays and Fridays involve planning and working with a flexible content calendar. My day-to-day work is accomplished mostly on Mondays and Fridays too. Tuesdays, Wednesdays, and Thursdays are meetings (Zooms) with clients—strategy meetings and setting the tone for the social media message. I meet with every client once a month for social medial planning. I am also creating new content and doing research on these days. I always have a buffer built in.

You have to be flexible and be able to rearrange your schedule. Social media by nature changes quickly and trends come up. Flexibility is key! Being able to juggle priorities is important as well.

What is the best part of being in this field?

It's never boring! You have to become a quick expert on a lot of different things, which can be a lot of fun. It can be challenging too. I also enjoy meeting people. You need people skills because you will deal with all different kinds of people.

The flexibility is really nice too. I can work from anywhere. Except for in-person meetings, I can arrange my schedule to work whenever it's best for me. I can be there for my kids when I need to. The constant variety is great. The creative aspect of it is great too.

I am naturally interested in news and current events and pop culture, and all of that comes in handy when you work with social media.

Do you think your education adequately prepared you for your current career path?

As much as it could at the time, I think so. If you want to be in communications of anything, you must be a good writer and a solid communicator. This is true in any profession really. My roles have naturally evolved, but the key skills of writing and communicating well are very important. It's not about posting neat pictures.

My education taught me the fundamentals of writing, which was important.

What has been most surprising about your career path?

Working in social media is not just sitting around posting. It's much more about strategizing and working with others. You have to make connections and develop relationships. There is a lot of work that goes on behind the scenes—brand development etcetera. You have to get information proactively. Social media bleeds into a lot of other things. The best SM managers have experience and can see the big picture and have knowledge of the other pieces.

It is much more time consuming than you think to create an effective brand and social media presence.

Everybody has access to websites and social media—so everyone is out there making noise. What needs to remain constant are the personal connections with people. Connecting to people emotionally sets you apart. It's fun to have a glossy approach, but you have to be authentic. If you're too fake, people will know or find out, and that only damages the brand. Authenticity is key.

Technology will shift and change, but knowing how to tell people stories will never be out of fashion.

What traits or skills make for a good digital communications professional?

If you want to be in communications in any field, you must be a good writer and a solid communicator. This is true in any profession really. My roles have naturally evolved, but the key skill of writing and communicating well is very important. It's not about posting neat pictures.

You need to be self-aware in this field too. There are many gray areas here— you must be aware of your own strengths and weaknesses and learn new things. The soft skills and having a high EQ (emotional quotient) are really important to be successful.

Making connections is very important too. You can't do all this on your own, especially when you are a freelancer. Networking is important—you want it to be natural for them to think of you when they have an issue.

You are sometimes in the role of customer service. You need the skills to do that successfully. Flexibility is also important. Having some data analysis skills is also important.

What advice do you have for young people considering this career? How can a young person prepare for this career while in high school?

Of course, stay up on the platforms that businesses use. Try to find a mentor that you can talk to. Making connections is important. Also follow different kinds of accounts that you think are good and see what they are doing.

Social media offers a lot of opportunities for young people to get their foot in the door. Try to get your feet wet at a small company your family knows so you can start to practice. When you build a little experience, you might find little jobs here and there to help small companies.

If you want to get into this career because you like posting pictures and you think that's fun, that's fine, but it won't be enough to sustain a career. Try to get even the most basic experience from a company. Learn as much as you can. Writing and communication skills are critical. You don't have to be an English professor, but hone your ability to write well in different ways.

Making High School Count

Regardless of the career you choose, there are some basic yet important things you can do while in high school to position yourself in the most advantageous way. Remember—it's not just about having the best application; it's also about figuring out which areas of digital communication you actually would enjoy doing and which ones don't suit you:

- Hone your communication skills in English, speech, and debate. You'll need them to speak with everyone: coworkers, clients, and bosses.
- Take classes in marketing and advertising.
- Be comfortable using all kinds of computer software.
- Volunteer in as many settings as you can. Read on to learn more about this important aspect of career planning.
- Take online courses in HTML, Cascading Style Sheets (CSS), JavaScript, the Adobe suite of products (Photoshop, Illustrator, InDesign, and Acrobat), and so on. You can find relatively inexpensive courses online and gain access to expensive software at a reduced, student rate (or use the versions at your high school).

Courses to Take in High School

Depending on your high school and what courses you have access to, there are many subjects that will help you prepare for a career in digital communications. If you go to a school that offers programming, marketing, journalism, or multimedia courses, those are good places to start. However, there are other courses and subjects that are just as relevant. Some of them may seem unrelated initially, but they will all help you prepare yourself and develop key skills:

- **Language arts:** Because team collaboration is the essence of a job in the digital communications industry, ensuring that you know how to communicate clearly and effectively—in both spoken and written language—will be key. It helps avoid unnecessary frustration, delays, financial and time costs, and errors if you can clearly convey and understand ideas.
- **Interpersonal communication/public speaking:** These courses will be an asset in any profession, including the digital communications industry. If you need to present ideas or results to your team, sales staff, or clients, these will be very important skills to hone.
- **Business and economics:** As with any type of business, if you have the ambition to run your own, knowledge gained in business and economics classes will prepare you to make smarter business and financial decisions.

- **Specialized software:** Digital communications specialists will need to be skilled in the technical tools they will use daily in their work. This could include tools as diverse as HTML, CSS, JavaScript, Google Analytics, audio editing software like Sound Forge, and the Adobe suite of products as well as multimedia apps and programs.

Gaining Work Experience

The best way to learn anything is to do it. When it comes to preparing for a career in digital communications, there are several options for gaining real-world experience and getting a feel for whether you are choosing the right career for you.

The one big benefit of jobs in the digital communications industry is that you don't have to land a work-experience opportunity at an established or upcoming company to prove what you've got and what you can do. Rather than wait for someone to invite you to work for them, you are wise to keep working on your own to show not only your talent but also your passion.

This means, for example, that you need to get out there and create a podcast with your friend about your favorite pastime, create a mock social media campaign for a favorite website or brand, or create some works on your own websites and build a strong portfolio. Be sure that you create works that are suitable to the market you want to get into.

TIPS FROM THE EXPERTS: CREATING A STANDOUT PORTFOLIO

If you decide that a portfolio is something you'll need to break into the digital communications field of your interest (it's not necessary in all cases), there are many online tools available—free and by subscription—that can help you. Your portfolio is an important part of your application, as it allows you not only to showcase your work but also to express who you are and how passionate you are about what you do. Your résumé is important, but your portfolio is where you really show your talent and your personal style.

Here are some of the main takeaways on creating your portfolio:

- Create your portfolio online and always keep your portfolio site up to date.
- Think about your audience when creating your portfolio.
- Don't distract from the work. Make your presentation about the work, not the interface.
- The fewer clicks it takes before your work is presented, the better.
- Make sure your images are relevant to the job you are applying for and don't be afraid to shuffle them to fit.
- Choose a platform and keep in mind that whichever platform you choose should be as customizable as possible so that you can keep your creative flow and stick to your brand.
- Make it easy to find you. Your contact info should be easily accessible from any point on your web page.
- Never stop creating. Revamp your site design every so often. Try to post something new as often as you can.
- Don't include anything but your very *best* work. Better a few pieces that rock than a wide variety of samples that make your work quality look variable.
- *Most important:* Always push yourself and get critiques and feedback from the most critical person you know.[1]

Come up with concepts that are related to the kind of digital communications you want to do. You can impress potential employers—or college entrance boards if you're still in high school—with your own ideas from your portfolio.

Educational Requirements

Depending on the type of job you want to pursue in digital communications, various levels of education are required. In some cases, it is possible to enter the field without a college degree—but to advance to higher levels within your career, a degree is usually preferred by employers. The general requirements in terms of education for all digital communications jobs are similar. A bachelor's degree or an associate degree in marketing or advertising, public relations, web design, communications, journalism, or a related field are all common ways that people begin careers as digital communications specialists.

On the two ends, web analytics specialists typically need more experience and perhaps a higher degree in marketing or business. Podcasters, on the other hand, can and often are self-taught as far as audio production goes. But even then, the more background and experience you have in marketing, advertising, and/or graphic design and media, the better situated you'll be to find a job.

> Search engines like Google are constantly innovating and modifying their code with the goal of ensuring that their users have a good experience on the site. When my clients ask about a particular feature or search engine recommendation, I need to make sure I've not only heard about it, but that I have an opinion on it before they ask. Keeping up with all the documentation can be a challenge.—Erik Dafforn, SEO analytics consultant

Next, we discuss the considerations to keep in mind when deciding what level of education is best for you to pursue. In chapter 3, we outline in more detail the types of programs offered.

WHY CHOOSE AN ASSOCIATE DEGREE

With a two-year degree—called an associate degree—you are qualified to apply for certain positions within digital communications. Common associate degrees offered that pertain to digital communications are in marketing, advertising, business, computer graphics, web design, public relations, communications, and even programming.

These degree programs are sufficient to give you a knowledge base to begin your career and can form a base should you decide to pursue a four-year degree later. Do keep in mind, though, that many jobs within the digital communications industry are quite competitive. With so much competition out there, the more of an edge you can give yourself, the better your chances will be.

Tip: Keep in mind that community colleges and technical schools can be a much cheaper way (as little as half the cost) to attain the same degree, and as long as those programs are accredited, it won't always matter to potential employers that you didn't attend a more recognizable university. Be sure to keep up with the news as well, as there is talk from the Biden administration about making community college free of charge.

WHY CHOOSE A BACHELOR'S DEGREE

A bachelor's degree—which usually takes four years to obtain—is a requirement for most careers related to the digital communications industry. In general, the higher the education you pursue, the better your odds are to advance in your career, which means more opportunity and, often, better compensation.

The difference between an associate and a bachelor's degree is of course the amount of time each takes to complete. To earn a bachelor's degree, a candidate must complete 40 college credits compared with 20 for an associate. This translates to more courses completed and a deeper exploration of degree content, even though similar content is covered in both.

Note: Even when not required, a bachelor's degree can help advance your career, give you an edge over the competition in the field, and earn you a higher starting salary than holders of an associate degree.

Another important conclusion to come to is whether you consider yourself a creative person who will learn the programs and applications needed to be creative or whether you're a technical person who wants to use technology to create things and be creative. This isn't a subtle difference when it comes to a career trajectory.

CHOOSING THE CREATIVE PATH

If you have the drive and talent to pursue being a digital artist/communicator, a bachelor's degree in fine arts, graphic design, or creative writing may be the best path for you. Then you will need to learn the programs and applications you need to be computer literate in your field. There are hundreds of postsecondary colleges, universities, and independent institutes in the United States with such programs. These types of programs include classes in fine art, principles of design, computerized design, commercial graphics production, fiction writing, printing techniques, and website design.[2]

CHOOSING THE TECHNICAL PATH

Another way to approach digital communications is from the computer science angle. Programs in digital communications often include courses in computer science in addition to marketing courses. If you know for sure that you want to be a multimedia artist or a content designer, having the technical education can be an asset. You still need to create unique ideas and projects, but those skills can be honed specifically for the kind of job you want.

Which path you take depends on your talents, your focus, and your ultimate career plans. You may find that you are initially more marketable if you get a computer graphics–related degree, but you might have to work harder to make sure you aren't pigeonholed into a technical job where you don't get to express your creativity. If you get a degree in art and design and you have the technical know-how, you have a better chance of being hired for your creative talents to begin with. But keep in mind that it's a highly competitive market to break into. And regardless of the path, you need experience, education, and skills in written and spoken communication.

No matter which path you choose, make sure the university or college you attend is properly accredited so that your degree will mean something to employers out in the real world.

The type of degree you decide to pursue is dependent on many factors, including your educational goals, career plans, and budget. Remember that there is no one right answer. *SvetaZi/iStock/Getty Images*

WHAT'S THE DIFFERENCE BETWEEN ACCREDITATION AND CERTIFICATION?

These terms can be confusing, and people often mess them up and use them incorrectly, contributing to the overall confusion. To clear it up, *accreditation* is the act of officially recognizing an organizational body, person, or educational facility as having a particular status or being qualified to perform a particular activity. For example, schools and colleges are accredited. *Certification*, on the other hand, is the process of confirming that a person has certain skills or knowledge. This is usually provided by some third-party review, assessment, or educational body. Individuals, not organizations, are certified. This also might be referred to as being *licensed*. Certification programs are generally available through software product vendors, such as Google. Such certifications can give you a competitive advantage over your peers.

Experience-Related Requirements

This section helps point you to ways in which you can gain helpful experience in the digital communications field before and during the time you're pursuing your education. This can and should start in high school, especially during the summers. Experience is important for many reasons, not the least of which are the following:

- Shadowing others in the profession can help reveal what the job is really like and whether it's something that you think you want to do day in and day out. This is a relatively risk-free way to explore different career paths. Ask any "seasoned" adult, and they will tell you that figuring out what you *don't* want to do is sometimes more important than figuring out what you *do* want to do.
- Internships and volunteer work are relatively quick ways to gain work experience and develop job skills.
- Volunteering can help you learn the intricacies of the profession, such as what types of environments are best and which skills you need to work on.

- Gaining experience during your high school years sets you apart from the many others who are applying to programs.
- Volunteering means that you'll be meeting many others doing the job that you might someday want to do (think career networking). You have the potential to develop mentor relationships, cultivate future job prospects, and get to know people who can recommend you for later positions.

Consider these tidbits of advice to maximize your volunteer experience.[3] They will help you stand out:

- Get diverse experiences. For example, try to shadow at least two different places of business.
- Try to gain 40 hours of volunteer experience in each setting. This is typically considered enough to show that you understand what a full workweek looks like in that setting. This can be as few as four to five hours per week over 10 weeks or so.
- Don't be afraid to ask questions. Just be considerate of others' time and wait until they are not busy to pursue your questions. Asking good questions shows that you have a real curiosity for the profession.
- Maintain and cultivate professional relationships. Write thank-you notes, send updates about your application progress, tell them where you decide to go to school, and check in occasionally. If you want to find a good mentor, you need to be a gracious and willing mentee.

Look at these kinds of experiences as ways to learn about the profession, show people how capable you are, and make connections to others that could last your career. It may even help you get into the college of your choice, and it will definitely help you write your *personal statement* that explains why you want to work in digital communications.

Another way to find a position (or at least a company that is open to curious students) is to start with their website. Visit the websites listed in this book and don't be afraid to pick up the phone and call local companies. Be prepared to start by making copies, assisting with clerical work, and other such tasks. No matter what you're doing, being on-site will teach you more than you know. With a great attitude and work ethic, you will likely be given more responsibility over time.

Networking

Because it's so important, a final word about networking is appropriate here. It's important to develop mentor relationships even at this stage. Remember that about 85 percent of jobs are found through personal contacts.[4] If you know someone in the field, don't hesitate to reach out. Be patient and polite but ask for help, perspective, and guidance.

Making connections to others in your prospective field is a great way to learn and be exposed to opportunity. *izusek/E+/Getty Images*

If you don't know anyone, ask your school guidance counselor to help you make connections or pick up the phone yourself. Reaching out with a genuine interest in knowledge and a real curiosity about the field will go a long way. You don't need a job or an internship just yet—only a connection that could blossom into a mentoring relationship. Follow these important but simple rules for the best results when networking:

- Do your homework about a potential contact, connection, university, school, or employer before you make contact. Be sure to have a general understanding of what they do and why. But don't be a know-it-all. Be open and ready to ask good questions.

- Be considerate of professionals' time and resources. Think about what they can get from you in return for mentoring or helping you.
- Speak and write with proper English. Proofread all your letters, e-mails, and texts. Think about how you will be perceived at all times.
- Always stay positive.
- Show your passion for the subject matter.

Summary

In this chapter, you learned even more about what it's like to work in digital communications. This chapter discussed the educational options of these different areas. You also learned about getting experience and creating your portfolio if needed. At this time, you should have a good idea of the schooling options and the paths you might consider taking. You may have even contemplated some questions about what kind of career path fits your strengths, time requirements, and wallet. Are you starting to picture your career plan? If not, that's okay, as there's still time.

Remember that no matter which of these areas you pursue, you must maintain your knowledge of the latest and greatest computer programs, applications, and programming languages used in your field. Advances in technology are frequent and constant, and it's vitally important that you keep apprised of what's happening in your field. The bottom line is that you need to have a lifelong love of learning to succeed in any digital field.

In chapter 3, we go into a lot more detail about pursuing the best educational path. The chapter covers how to find the best value for your education and includes a discussion about financial aid and scholarships. At the end of the chapter, you should have a clearer view of the educational landscape and how and where you fit in.

Pursuing the Education Path

*W*hen it comes time to start looking at colleges, universities, or postsec-ondary schools, many high schoolers tend to freeze up at the enormity of the job ahead of them. This chapter will help break down this process for you so that it won't seem so daunting.

Yes, finding the right college or learning institution is an important one, and it's a big step toward achieving your career goals and dreams. Chapter 2 covered the various educational requirements of the digital communications field, which means you should now be ready to find an institution of learning. This isn't always simply a process of finding the very best school that you can afford and be accepted into, although that might end up being your path. It should also be about finding the right fit so that you can have the best possible experience during your post–high school years.

It's important to find a postsecondary school that fits your needs and budget. *martinedoucet/ E+/Getty Images*

The truth is that postsecondary schooling isn't only about getting a degree. It's also about learning how to be an adult, managing your life and your responsibilities, being exposed to new experiences, growing as a person, and otherwise moving toward becoming an adult who contributes to society. College—in whatever form it takes for you—offers you an opportunity to actually become an interesting person with perspective on the world and empathy and consideration for people other than yourself.

An important component of how successful college will be for you is finding the right fit—the right school that brings out the best in you and challenges you at different levels. I know, no pressure, right? Just as with finding the right profession, your ultimate goal should be to match your personal interests, goals, and personality with the college's goals and perspective. For example, small liberal arts colleges have a much different "feel" and philosophy than Big Ten or PAC-12 state schools. And rest assured that all this advice applies even when you're planning on attending community college or another postsecondary school.

Don't worry, though. In addition to these "soft skills," this chapter does dive into the nitty-gritty of finding the best schools no matter what you want to do.

WHAT IS A GAP YEAR?

Taking a year off between high school and college, often called a gap year, is normal, perfectly acceptable, and almost required in many countries throughout the world, and it is becoming increasingly acceptable in the United States as well. Even Malia Obama, former President Obama's daughter, did it. Because the cost of college has gone up dramatically, it literally pays for you to know going in what you want to study, and a gap year—well spent—can do lots to help you answer that question.

Some great ways to spend your gap year include joining the Peace Corps or AmeriCorps organizations, enrolling in a mountaineering program or other gap year–styled program, backpacking across Europe or other countries on the cheap (be safe and bring a friend), finding a volunteer organization that furthers a cause you believe in or that complements your career aspirations, joining a Road Scholar program (see www.roadscholar.org), teaching English in another country (see https://www

.gooverseas.com/blog/best-countries-for-seniors-to-teach-english-abroad for more information), or working and earning money for college.

Many students will find that they get much more out of college when they have a year to mature and to experience the real world. The Gap Year Association reports from their alumni surveys that students who take gap years show improved civic engagement, improved college graduation rates, and improved grade-point averages (GPAs) in college.[1] You can use your gap year to explore and solidify your thoughts and plans about a career in digital communications as well as to add impressive experiences to your college application.

See the Gap Year Association website at https://gapyearassociation.org for lots of advice and resources if you're considering a potentially life-altering experience.

Finding the College That's Right for You

Before you look into which schools have the degree(s) you're interested in, it will behoove you to take some time to consider what "type" of school will be best for you. If nothing else, answering questions like the following ones can help you narrow your search and focus on a smaller sampling of choices. Write down your answers to these questions so that you can refer to them often, such as in the Notes app on your phone:

- **Size:** Does the size of the school matter to you? Colleges and universities range from 500 or fewer students to 25,000 students.
- **Community location:** Would you prefer to be in a rural area, a small town, a suburban area, or a large city? How important is the location of the school in the larger world to you?
- **Distance from home:** Will you live at home to save money? If not, how far away from home do you want or are willing to go? Phrase this in terms of hours away or miles away.
- **Housing options:** What kind of housing would you prefer? Dorms, off-campus apartments, and private homes are all common options.
- **Student body:** How would you like the student body to "look"? Think about coed versus all-male and all-female settings as well as the makeup

of minorities, how many students are part-time versus full-time, and the percentage of commuter students. Who will you likely meet there?

- **Academic environment:** Consider which majors are offered and at which levels of degree. Research the student-to-faculty ratio. Are the classes taught by professors or more often by teaching assistants? Find out how many internships the school typically provides to students. Are independent study or study abroad programs available in your area of interest?

- **Financial aid availability/cost:** Does the school provide ample opportunities for scholarships, grants, work-study programs, and the like? Does cost play a role in your options (for most people, it does)?

- **Support services:** Investigate the strength of the academic and career placement counseling services of the school.

- **Social activities and athletics:** Does the school offer clubs that you are interested in? Which sports are offered? Are scholarships available?

- **Specialized programs:** Does the school offer honors programs or programs for veterans or students with disabilities or special needs?

> Knowledge is indivisible. When people grow wise in one direction, they are sure to make it easier for themselves to grow wise in other directions as well. On the other hand, when they split up knowledge, concentrate on their own field, and scorn and ignore other fields, they grow less wise, even in their own field.—Isaac Asimov[2]

Not all of these questions are going to be important to you, and that's fine. Be sure to make note of aspects that don't matter so much to you too, such as size or location. You might change your mind as you go to visit colleges, but it's important to make note of where you're at to begin with.

Consider the School's Reputation

One factor in choosing a college or certificate program is the school's reputation. This reputation is based on the quality of education previous students have had there. If you go to a school with a healthy reputation in your field, it gives potential employers a place to start when they are considering your credentials and qualifications.

Factors vary depending on which schools offer the program you want, so take these somewhat lightly. Some of the factors affecting reputation generally include the following:

- **Nonprofit or for-profit:** In general, schools that are nonprofit (or not-for-profit) organizations have better reputations than for-profit schools. In fact, it's best to avoid for-profit schools.
- **Accreditation:** Your program must be accredited by a regional accrediting body to be taken seriously in the professional world. It would be very rare to find an unaccredited college or university with a good reputation.
- **Acceptance rate:** Schools that accept a very high percentage of applicants can have lower reputations than those that accept a smaller percentage. That's because a high acceptance rate can indicate that there isn't much competition for those spaces or that standards are not as high.
- **Alumni:** What have graduates of the program gone on to do? The college's or department's website can give you an idea of what their graduates are doing.
- **History:** Schools that have been around a long time tend to be doing something right. They also tend to have good alumni networks, which can help you when you're looking for a job or a mentor.
- **Faculty:** Schools with a high percentage of permanent faculty versus adjunct faculty tend to have better reputations. Bear in mind that if you're going to a specialized program or certification program, this might be reversed—these programs are frequently taught by experts who are working in the field.
- **Departments:** A department at one school might have a better reputation than a similar department at a school that's more highly ranked overall. If the department you'll be attending is well known and respected, that could be more important than the overall reputation of the institution itself.

There are a lot of websites that claim to have the "top 10 schools" for this and that. It's hard to tell which of those are truly accurate. So where do you begin? *U.S. News & World Report* is a great place to start to find a college or university with a great reputation. Go to www.usnews.com/education to find links to the highest-ranked schools for the undergraduate or graduate degree programs you're interested in.

LISA A. BUCKI, AUTHOR, TRAINER, AND CONTENT EXPERT

Lisa A. Bucki. *Courtesy of Lisa A. Bucki*

Lisa A. Bucki received her bachelor's degree in public and corporate communications from Butler University in Indianapolis. She started her career in public relations (PR) working for a PR firm before transitioning to computer book publishing in the late 1980s.

She's an author, trainer, and content expert and has been educating others about computers, software, business, and personal growth topics since 1990. She has written and contributed to dozens of books and multimedia works in addition to providing marketing and training services to her clients and writing online tutorials. Bucki is cofounder of 1x1 Media, LLC (www.1x1media .com), an independent publisher of books and courses focused on how-to topics for entrepreneurs, start-up founders, makers, and other business professionals.

Can you explain how you ended up in the digital communications field? What about it interested you?

The digital side for me has been largely self-taught, although I took a general computing course at Butler University. Later, when working for a PR firm, I was the least intimidated by the emerging technology. We had a client or two who wanted a newsletter template that they could then modify themselves. I was sent to teach clients like that how to use PageMaker.

As a kid, I had a TI-99 game console, which you could also program on. I wrote a program to balance a checkbook in BASIC. Essentially, I had an affinity for computers, and I think my brain was organized like a computer. So part of it was interest, and part was a natural affinity.

What's a "typical" day in your job? What do you do, day to day?

I normally have a reading and research period in the morning when I check in with industry resources. I keep my knowledge of the field up to date, such as knowing the timing of major Windows updates, 5G, and other new technologies rolling out.

My heavy work period is in the afternoon, where I can focus and concentrate for a longer period of time. A large block of continuous work time is important for productivity and consistency. I am primarily writing and creating content during this time. I do some technical editing as well. In some cases, my husband and I discuss projects or opportunities that we have coming up for 1x1 Media. I also am active on social media promoting our 1x1 Media products. We monitor our general information e-mail address for user messages and comments. We also look at our book listings on Amazon to see how well they are being received, check and respond to reviews, and check our sales information.

What is the best part of being in the digital communications field? Is it what you expected it would be?

The digital world has enabled me to have this independent career that I could not have envisioned as a young person.

What I continue to like about it is that I get to try out new technologies—hardware, software, platforms, and ways of working. I like digital tools that help you work smarter. When I am on my smartphone, I am being productive. I am a "work smarter, not harder" person, and I think technologies can help you do that now more than ever.

The continuous ongoing rate of change is surprising to me. Hardware and software are both obsolete so much more quickly now. Good internet connectivity in rural areas is a critical issue as well. This can be a challenge for all. Having the right systems and tools in place is critical.

What's the greatest challenge the market faces at this time?

The educational publishing world seems to be struggling with getting the combination of print and digital right so that students can use the materials effectively and so each offering seems like a good value. Many, many people are fine with using subscription services for music now (even though there was initial resistance), and perhaps publishing will move that way. How well publishers manage these transitions continues to be a challenge.

As far as other digital markets, the proliferation of apps makes it a challenge for developers to gain traction and get an audience. It takes a lot more investment to get it going. And how does social media fit in? What do we do when someone is not using the platform appropriately? Do these offerings make society better or worse?

Do you think your education adequately prepared you for your current career path?

As for the writing side, it definitely did. I took business courses and lots of different writing classes: essay writing, journalism, marketing, speechwriting, and other writing classes. These were all very constructive for my future career. I would have taken some coding or programming if I knew I would end up in technical writing. That would have opened up doors for me in the digital field. If you are maintaining a website created using WordPress, for example, you have to know at least a little about HTML coding. You need coding skills *and* writing skills to communicate effectively in this career space, where technology and education intersect. Digital content development also requires some experience with various technical skills.

Where do you see this field going in the future?

I believe this field will become more important because all jobs are being transformed by digital technology, which means the need to coherently convey how-to information will become more and more important. In the ever-noisier digital universe, a person who can craft a good message and deliver it to the right audience will always be in demand.

What traits or skills make for a good digital communications professional?

Top of my list is the ability to communicate effectively by e-mail and text! I have had experience with people who have difficulty saying what they really mean or not being good at reading and fully answering e-mail messages or endlessly responding to an e-mail without editing the subject line. Self-discipline is very important, which can mean *not* communicating sometimes. Edit yourself before you send out a message. The internet is forever.

If you want to work independently, you need a disciplined routine. This doesn't mean working 12 hours a day, but a routine is important. You have to do the work and have a schedule.

Other things like coding and other technical skills are important. Leading by helping others and sharing your technical skills is also key. These both can open career opportunities for you.

What advice do you have for young people considering this career? How can a young person prepare for this career while in high school?

Seek out opportunities like online coding camps and seminars. Look for mentors who can help you—whether that's fellow students, professors, or a career professional. Some areas have networking groups for digital content fields—find out if you have one of those in your area and join it. You can network and exchange ideas there.

There are also many free and degree-related online courses on these digital topics as well. It's not a bad idea to get certifications, badges, and credentials in your areas of interest.

Unless you have a passion for one specific area, I think it's better to have more than just one core skill. I use writing *and* technical skills, not just one or the other. Be aware that multiple skill sets go together in many careers. For example, data analysis often involves math aptitude, coding, writing, and strong attention to detail.

Finally, if you want to be independent, at least learn the basics of business accounting so you can keep a handle on your finances. Know about self-employment tax and other financial elements of running a business. As the old saying goes, if you take care of your money, your money will take care of you!

Any last thoughts?

Take a basic touch-typing class if you plan on writing a lot. There are many online courses and tools that teach this skill. Learn to type first. You'll be glad you did.

After the Research, Trust Your Gut

U.S. News & World Report puts it best when they say the college that fits you best is one that will do all these things:

- Offers a degree that matches your interests and needs
- Provides a style of instruction that matches the way you like to learn
- Provides a level of academic rigor to match your aptitude and preparation
- Offers a community that feels like home to you
- Values you for what you do well[3]

Note: According to the National Center for Education Statistics, which is part of the U.S. Department of Education, six years after entering college for an undergraduate degree, only 60 percent of students will have graduated.[4] Barely half of those students will graduate from college in their lifetime.[5] By the same token, it's never been more important to get your degree. College graduates with a bachelor's degree typically earn 66 percent more than those with only a high school diploma and are also far less likely to face unemployment. Also, over the course of a lifetime, the average worker with a bachelor's degree will earn approximately $1 million more than a worker without a postsecondary education.[6]

As you look at the facts and figures, you also need to think about a less quantifiable aspect of choosing a college or university: *fit*. What does that mean? It's hard to describe, but students know it when they feel it. It means finding the school that not only offers the program you want but also feels right. Many students have no idea what they're looking for in a school until they walk onto the campus for a visit. Suddenly, they'll say to themselves, "This is the one!"

Touring the campus and talking to current students are really important. *SDI Productions/E+/Getty Images*

While you're evaluating a particular institution's offerings with your conscious mind, your unconscious mind is also at work, gathering information about all kinds of things at lightning speed. When it tells your conscious mind what it's decided, we call that a "gut reaction." Pay attention to your gut reactions. There's good information in there.

It is hoped that this section has emphasized the importance of finding the right college fit. Take some time to paint a mental picture about the kind of university or school setting that will best meet your needs.

Note: According to the U.S. Department of Education,[7] as many as 32 percent of college students transfer colleges during the course of their educational career—that is, the decision you initially make is not set in stone. Do your best to make a good choice but remember that you can change your mind, your major, and even your campus. Many students do it and go on to have great experiences and earn great degrees.

Honing Your Degree Plan

This section outlines the different approaches you can take to get a degree that will land you your dream job in digital communications, whether it be as a content creator, podcaster, digital media marketer, web analytics specialist, or something related to all of these.

RELEVANT DEGREE PATHS TO CONSIDER

As you've no doubt learned if you've read this far into the book, the digital communications umbrella has many varied but related professions within it. No matter which area you want to focus on, having at least an associate degree (a two-year degree) is going to give you a leg up during the interviewing process. The good news is that your degree can be in a variety of areas, including marketing, advertising, business, journalism, graphic design, public relations, or even something as specific as digital communications. Consider these points:

- As an associate degree is a two-year process, it's cheaper and takes less time. Many digital communications professionals start their careers with associate degrees in any entry-level position. Once you are hired, you may be in a position to have your employer pay for you to get your bachelor's degree.
- If you want to enter the workforce in web analytics or doing data interpretation and visualization, you'll likely need a bachelor's degree (a four-year degree). This could be in computer or information science, communications, business, marketing, or advertising.

So what does the typical marketing degree require of you? As a sampling, the typical business/marketing student usually takes the following classes:

- Business-to-business (B2B) marketing
- Marketing research
- Marketing strategy and management
- Internet marketing and advertising
- E-commerce

A typical computer design degree, on the other hand, will offer courses on the following subjects:

- Introduction to computer graphics
- Computer animation
- Computer programming
- Digital modeling
- Graphic design
- 3D design

A typical digital communications/journalism degree, on the other hand, will offer courses on the following subjects:

- Digital media arts
- Corporate communication/public relations
- Feature writing
- Creative writing
- Digital animation
- Information systems management

These are just samples of what you will take to gain a degree. Be sure to check the curricula of the schools you're considering attending for more specific information. The point is that you can choose among several different majors if you want a career in digital communications.

Starting Your College Search

If you're currently in high school and are serious about working in the digital communications field, start by finding four or five schools in a realistic location (for you) that offer the degree you're interested in. Not every school that is near you or that you have an initial interest in will offer the degree you desire, so narrow your choices accordingly. With that said, consider attending a public university in your resident state, if possible, as this will save you lots of money. Private institutions don't typically discount resident student tuition costs. Be sure to research the basic GPA and Scholastic Aptitude Test (SAT) or American College Test (ACT) requirements of each school as well.

Tip: For those of you applying to associate degree programs or greater, most advisers recommend that students take both the ACT and the SAT during their junior year (spring at the latest). (The ACT is generally considered more weighted in science, so take that into consideration.) You can retake these tests and use your highest score, so be sure to leave time to retake early in your senior year if needed. You want your best score to be available to all the schools you're applying to by January 1 of your senior year. The score can then be considered with any of your scholarship applications (unless you want to do *early decision*, which can provide you with certain benefits). Remember that these are general time lines—be sure to check the exact deadlines and calendars of the schools to which you're applying. See the section "Know the Deadlines" later in this chapter for more information about various deadlines.

Once you have found four or five schools in a realistic location for you that offer the degree you want to pursue, spend some time on their websites studying the requirements for admissions. Most universities will list the average statistics for the last class accepted to the program. Important factors weighing on your decision of what schools to apply to should include whether you meet the requirements, your chances of getting in (but shoot high), tuition costs, availability of scholarships and grants, location, and the school's reputation and licensure/graduation rates.

Note: Most colleges and universities will list the average statistics for the last class accepted to the program, which will give you a sense of your chances of acceptance.

The order of these characteristics will depend on your grades and test scores, your financial resources, and other personal factors. You want to find a university with a good degree program and one that also matches your academic rigor and practical needs.

Choosing a Major

Chapter 2 discusses in some detail how many different majors you could pursue if you wanted to end up in the digital communications field. There are many, and it depends on what field you're interested in. A bachelor's degree in marketing, advertising, or a related field is a great option. However, some people choose a more general degree, such as business or communications, which may provide you with a more well-rounded education. Others tend toward journalism or something more creative, like graphic design. Or you could instead obtain a degree in computer graphics and work on your creativity from that standpoint. The good news is that there are many degree paths you can take to end up with a career in digital communications. It all depends on your interests and the degrees that appeal most to you.

Regardless of the field of study you choose, you'll need strong technical and communication skills to succeed. Certification programs are available through software product vendors, such as Google. Certification in certain software programs demonstrates competence and may provide you with a competitive advantage.

CREATING A PORTFOLIO

Whether you need to create a portfolio depends on the area of digital communications you want to focus on. If your focus is on content creation, podcasting, or any other creative aspect of digital communications, it might not be a bad idea to build a portfolio of your work.

Your portfolio should showcase your best work. At different times in your life, it will contain different types of work, depending on what you're using it for. If you are applying to school, your portfolio should be a broad representation of your best work in the various media you use.

So what should your portfolio contain? Different schools will have some different requirements, but in general you want to showcase the following:[8]

- Ten to 20 examples of your absolute best work—think of your portfolio as your greatest hits
- Go for variety—showcase the different media you work in
- Personal work—pieces that come from your life or experiences in a way that's meaningful to you
- Your most original work—show them your ideas and what you will bring to the experience
- Anything else a specific school has asked you to include, such as your sketchbook

Your portfolio should consist mostly of finished work. Make sure your site is clean and easy to navigate. Don't make people dig through the site to find your work.

Applying and Getting Admitted

Once you've narrowed down your list of potential schools, of course, you'll want to be accepted. First, you need to apply.

There isn't enough room in this book to include everything you need to know about applying to colleges. But here is some useful information to get you started. Remember that every college and university is unique, so be sure to be in touch with their admissions offices so you don't miss any special requirements or deadlines.

APPLYING TO COLLEGES

It's a good idea to make yourself a "to do" list while you're a junior in high school. Already a senior? Already graduated? No problem. It's never too late to start.

Before you go to college, you have to be admitted. *twinsterphoto/iStock/Getty Images*

MAKE THE MOST OF SCHOOL VISITS

If it's at all practical and feasible, you should visit the schools you're considering. To get a real feel for any college or school, you need to walk around the campus and buildings, spend some time in the common areas where students hang out, and sit in on a few classes. You can also sign up for campus tours, which are typically given by current students. This is another good way to see the school and ask questions of someone who knows. Be sure to visit the specific school or building that covers your possible major as well. The website and brochures won't be able to convey that intangible feeling you'll get from a visit. (If you can't get there, check out their virtual tours online. Many more schools are providing in-depth campus, dorm, and building tours, especially due to COVID-19.)

In addition to the questions listed in the section "Finding the College That's Right for You" earlier in this chapter, consider these questions as well. Make a list of questions that are important to you before you visit:

- What is the makeup of the current freshman class? Is the campus diverse?

- What is the meal plan like? What are the food options?
- Where do most of the students hang out between classes? (Be sure to visit this area.)
- How long does it take to walk from one end of the campus to the other?
- What types of transportation are available for students? Does campus security provide escorts to cars, dorms, and so on at night?

To be ready for your visit and make the most of it before you go, consider these tips and words of advice:

- Be sure to do some research. At the least, spend some time on the college website. Make sure your questions aren't adequately addressed there first.
- Make a list of questions.
- Arrange to meet with a professor in your area of interest or to visit the specific school.
- Be prepared to answer questions about yourself and why you are interested in this school.
- Dress in neat, clean, and casual clothes. Avoid overly wrinkled clothing or anything with stains.
- Listen and take notes.
- Don't interrupt.
- Be positive and energetic.
- Make eye contact when someone speaks directly to you.
- Ask questions.
- Thank people for their time.

Finally, be sure to send thank-you notes or e-mails after the visit is over. Remind the recipient when you visited the campus and thank him or her for his or her time.

Standardized Tests

Many colleges and universities require scores from standardized tests that are supposed to measure your readiness for college and ability to succeed. There is debate about how accurate these tests are, so some institutions don't ask for them anymore. But most do, so you should expect to take them.

Undergraduate-Level Tests

To apply to an undergraduate program, students generally take either the SAT or the ACT. Both cover reading, writing, and math. Both have optional essays. Both are accepted by colleges and universities. Both take nearly the same amount of time to complete. If one test is preferred over another by schools, it's usually more about where you live than about the test.[9]

- **SAT:** Offered by the CollegeBoard.org. There are 20 SAT subject tests that you can take to show knowledge of special areas, such as math 1 and math 2, biology (ecological or molecular), chemistry, physics, as well as U.S. or world history and numerous languages.
- **ACT:** Offered by ACT.org. There aren't any subject tests available with the ACT. Questions are a little easier on the ACT, but you don't have as much time to answer them.

Ultimately, which test you take comes down to personal preference. Many students choose to take both exams.

Graduate-Level Tests

- **Graduate Record Exam (GRE):** Published by the Educational Testing Service (ETS). The GRE is the most widely used admission test for graduate and professional schools. It covers verbal and quantitative reasoning and analytical writing. The test results are considered along with your undergraduate record for admissions decisions to most graduate programs.
- **GRE subject tests:** Some graduate programs also want to see scores from subject tests. GRE subject tests are offered in biology, chemistry, English literature, mathematics, physics, and psychology.
- **Medical College Admission Test (MCAT):** Administered by the Association of American Medical Colleges (AAMC). MCAT is the standardized test for admission to medical school programs in allopathic, osteopathic, podiatric, or veterinary medicine (some veterinary programs accept the GRE instead).
- **Law School Admission Test (LSAT):** Administered by the Law School Admission Council seven times a year. This test for prospective law

school candidates is the only test accepted for admission purposes by all American Bar Association–accredited law schools and Canadian common-law law schools.

Know the Deadlines

- *Early decision (ED)* deadlines are usually in November, with acceptance decisions announced in December. Note that if you apply for ED admission and are accepted, that decision is binding, so apply ED only if you know exactly which school you want to go to and are ready to commit.
- *ED II* is a second round of early decision admissions. Not every school that does ED will also have an ED II. For those that do, deadlines are usually in January with decisions announced in February.
- *Regular decision* deadlines can be as early as January 1 but can go later. Decision announcements usually come out between mid-March and early April.
- *Rolling admission* is used by some schools. Applications are accepted at any time, and decisions are announced on a regular schedule. Once the incoming class is full, admissions for that year will close.

The Common Application

The Common Application form is a single, detailed application form that is accepted by more than 900 colleges and universities in the United States. Instead of filling out a different application form for every school you want to apply to, you fill out one form and have it sent to all the schools you're interested in. The Common Application itself is free, and most schools don't charge for submitting it.

If you don't want to use the Common Application for some reason, most colleges will also let you apply with a form on their website. There are a few institutions that want you to apply only through their sites and other highly regarded institutions that accept only the Common Application. Be sure you know what the schools you're interested in prefer.

The Common Application's website (www.commonapp.org) has a lot of useful information, including tips for first-time applicants and for transfer students.

Essays

Part of many college applications is a written essay, sometimes even two or three. Some colleges provide writing prompts they want you to address. The Common Application has numerous prompts that you can choose from. Here are some issues to consider when writing your essays:

- **Topic:** Choose something that has some meaning for you and that you can speak to in a personal way. This is your chance to show the college or university who you are as an individual. It doesn't have to be about an achievement or success, and it shouldn't be your whole life story. Maybe a topic relates to a time you learned something or had an insight into yourself.
- **Timing:** Start working on your essays the summer before senior year if possible. You won't have a lot of other homework in your way, and you'll have time to prepare thoughtful comments and polish your final essay.
- **Length:** Aim for between 250 and 650 words. The Common Application leans toward the long end of that range, while individual colleges might lean toward the shorter end.
- **Writing:** Use straightforward language. Don't turn in your first draft; rather, work on your essay and improve it as you go. Ask someone else to read it and tell you what they think. Ask your English teacher to look at it and make suggestions. Do *not* let someone else write any portion of your essay. Your essay needs to be *your* ideas and *your* writing to represent *you*.
- **Proofing:** Make sure your essay doesn't have any obvious errors. Run the spell-checker but don't trust it to find everything (spell-checkers are notorious for introducing weird errors). Have someone you trust read it over for you and note spelling, grammar, and other mistakes. Nobody can proofread their own work and find every mistake—what you'll see is what you expect to see. Even professional editors need other people to proofread their writing, so don't be embarrassed to ask for help.

Letters of Recommendation

Most college applications ask for letters of recommendation from people who know you well and can speak to what you're like as a student and as a person. How many you need varies from school to school, so check with the admissions office website to see what they want. Some schools don't want any.

Whom Should You Ask for a Letter?

Some schools will tell you pretty specifically whom they want to hear from. Others leave it up to you. Choose people who know you and think well of you, for example, the following:

- One or two teachers of your best academic subjects (English, math, science, social studies, etc.)
- Teacher of your best elective subject (art, music, media, etc.)
- Adviser for a club you're active in
- School counselor
- School principal (but only if you've taken a class with him or her or he or she knows you individually as a student)
- Community member you've worked with (scout leader, volunteer group leader, religious leader, etc.)
- Boss at a job you've held

When Should You Ask for a Letter?

Don't wait until applications are due. Give people plenty of time to prepare a good recommendation letter for you. If possible, ask for these letters in the late spring or early summer of your junior year.

Submitting Your Letters of Recommendation

Technically, you're not supposed to read your recommendation letters. That lets recommenders speak more freely about you. Some might show you the letter anyway, but that's up to them. Don't ask to see it.

Recommenders can submit their letters electronically either directly to the institutions you're applying to or through the Common Application. Your job is to be sure they know the submission deadlines well in advance so that they can send in the letters on time.

Admissions Requirements

Each college or university will have its own admissions requirements. In addition, the specific program or major you want to go into may have admissions requirements of its own in addition to the institution's requirements.

It's your responsibility to go to each institution's website and be sure you know and understand their requirements. That includes checking out each department site, too, to find any special prerequisites or other things that they're looking for.

THE MOST PERSONAL OF PERSONAL STATEMENTS

The *personal statement* you include with your application to college is extremely important, especially when your GPA and SAT/ACT scores are on the border of what is typically accepted. Write something that is thoughtful and that conveys your understanding of the information technology profession as well as your desire to work in the information technology world. Why are you uniquely qualified? Why are you a good fit for this university and program or these types of students? These essays should be highly personal (the "personal" in "personal statement"). Will the admissions professionals who read it, along with hundreds of others, come away with a snapshot of who you really are and what you are passionate about?

Look online for some examples of good personal statements that will give you a feel for what works. Be sure to check your specific school for length guidelines, format requirements, and any other guidelines they expect you to follow. Most important, make sure your passion for your potential career comes through—although make sure it is also genuine.

And, of course, be sure to proofread it several times and ask a professional (such as your school writing center or your local library services) to proofread it as well.

What's It Going to Cost You?

So, the bottom line—what will your education end up costing you? That depends on many factors, including the type and length of degree, where you attend (in state or not, private or public institution), how much in scholarships or financial aid you're able to obtain, your family or personal income, and many other factors.

The College Entrance Examination Board (see www.collegeboard.org) tracks and summarizes financial data from colleges and universities all over the United States. A sample of the most recent data is shown in the following table. It represents the state of things for the 2020–2021 academic year. (It's worth noting that these numbers represent a 2.5 percent increase over 2019–2020 costs before adjusting for inflation.) Costs shown are for one year.

Table 3.1. Average Estimated Full-Time Undergraduate Budgets (Enrollment Weighted) by Sector, 2020–2021[10]

Figure CP-1. Average Estimated Full-Time Undergraduate Budgets (Enrollment-Weighted) by Sector, 2020-21						
	Tuition and Fees	Room and Board	Books and Supplies	Transportation	Other Expenses	Total
Private Nonprofit Four-Year On-Campus	$37,650	$13,120	$1,240	$1,060	$1,810	$54,880
Public Four-Year Out-of-State On-Campus	$27,020	$11,620	$1,240	$1,230	$2,170	$43,280
Public Four-Year In-State On-Campus	$10,560	$11,620	$1,240	$1,230	$2,170	$26,820
Public Two-Year In-District Commuter	$3,770	$9,080	$1,460	$1,840	$2,400	$18,550

NOTES: Expense categories are based on institutional budgets for students as reported in the College Board's Annual Survey of Colleges. Figures for tuition and fees and room and board mirror those reported in Table 1. Books and supplies may include the cost of a personal computer used for study. Other expense categories are the average amounts allotted in determining the total cost of attendance and do not necessarily reflect actual student expenditures.

SOURCES: College Board, Annual Survey of Colleges; NCES, IPEDS Fall 2018 Enrollment data.

This table was prepared in October 2020.

> College may seem expensive. But the truth is that most students pay less than their college's sticker price, or published price, thanks to financial aid. So instead of looking at the published price, concentrate on your net price—the real price you'll pay for a college. . . . Your net price is a college's sticker price for tuition and fees minus the grants, scholarships, and education tax benefits you receive. The net price you pay for a particular college is specific to you because it's based on your personal circumstances and the college's financial aid policies.—College Board[11]

Keep in mind that these are averages and reflect the published prices, not the net prices. As an example of net cost, in 2019–2020, full-time in-state students at public four-year colleges must cover an average of about $15,400 in tuition and fees and room and board after grant aid and tax benefits in addition to paying for books and supplies and other living expenses.[12]

If you read more specific data about a particular university or find averages in your particular area of interest, you should assume that those numbers are closer to reality than these averages, as they are more specific. Such data show you the ballpark figures.

Generally, there is about a 3 percent annual increase in tuition and associated costs to attend college. In other words, if you are expecting to attend college two years after these data were collected, you need to add approximately 6 percent to these numbers. Keep in mind that this assumes no financial aid or scholarships of any kind (so it's not the net cost).

This chapter also covers finding the most affordable path to get the degree you want. Later in this section, you'll also learn how to prime the pumps and get as much money for college as you can.

Financial Aid

Finding the money to attend college, whether for two or four years, in an online program, or for a vocational career, can seem overwhelming. But you can do it if you have a plan before you actually start applying to college.

NOT ALL FINANCIAL AID IS CREATED EQUAL

Educational institutions tend to define financial aid as any scholarship, grant, loan, or paid employment that helps students pay their college expenses. Notice that financial aid covers both *money you have to pay back* and *money you don't have to pay back.* That's a big difference. Financial aid that does not need to be repaid includes the following:

- Grants
- Scholarships
- Work-study

Financial aid that does need to be repaid, with interest, includes the following:

- Federal government loans
- Private loans
- Institutional loans

If you get into your top-choice university, don't let the sticker price turn you away. Financial aid can come from many different sources, and it's available to cover all different kinds of costs you'll encounter during your years in college, including tuition, fees, books, housing, and food.

Paying for college can take a creative mix of grants, scholarships, and loans, but you can find your way with some help. *Rawpixel/iStock/Getty Images*

The good news is that universities more often offer incentive or tuition discount aid to encourage students to attend. The market is often more competitive in favor of the student, and colleges and universities are responding by offering more generous aid packages to a wider range of students than they used to. Here are some basic tips and pointers about the financial aid process:

- Apply for financial aid during your senior year. You must fill out the FAFSA (Free Application for Federal Student Aid) form, which can be filed starting October 1 of your senior year until June of the year you graduate.[13] Because the amount of available aid is limited, it's best to apply as soon as possible. To get started, visit https://studentaid.gov/h /apply-for-aid/fafsa.
- Be sure to compare and contrast deals you get at different schools. There is room to negotiate with universities. The first offer for aid may not be the best you'll get.
- Wait until you receive all offers from your top schools and then use this information to negotiate with your top choice to see if they will match or beat the best aid package you received.
- To be eligible to keep and maintain your financial aid package, you must meet certain grade/GPA requirements. Be sure you are very clear on these academic expectations and keep up with them.
- You must reapply for federal aid every year.

Tip: Watch out for scholarship scams. You should never be asked to pay to submit the FAFSA form ("free" is in its name) or be required to pay a lot to find appropriate aid and scholarships. These are free services. If an organization promises you that you'll get aid or that you have to "act now or miss out," these are warning signs of a less reputable organization.

Also, be careful with your personal information to avoid identity theft as well. Simple things like closing and exiting your browser after visiting sites where you entered personal information (like the FAFSA site) goes a long way. Don't share your student aid ID number with anyone either.

It's important to understand the different forms of financial aid that are available to you. That way, you'll know how to apply for different kinds and get the best financial aid package that fits your needs and strengths. The two main categories of financial aid are *gift aid*, which doesn't have to be repaid, and *self-help aid*, which consists of either loans that must be repaid or work-study funds that are earned. The next sections cover the various types of financial aid that fit in one of these areas.

GRANTS

Grants typically are awarded to students who have financial need but can also be used in the areas of athletics, academics, demographics, veteran support, and special talents. They do not have to be paid back. Grants can come from federal agencies, state agencies, specific universities, and private organizations. Most federal and state grants are based on financial need. Examples of grants are the Pell Grant and the SMART Grant.

SCHOLARSHIPS

Scholarships are merit-based aid that does not have to be paid back. They are typically awarded on the basis of academic excellence or some other special talent, such as music or art. Scholarships also fall under the areas of athletics, aid for minorities women, and so on. These are typically not awarded by federal or state governments but instead come from the specific school you applied to as well as private and nonprofit organizations.

Be sure to reach out directly to the financial aid officers of the schools you want to attend. These people are great contacts and can lead you to many more sources of scholarships and financial aid. For more information about how scholarships in general work, visit www.gocollege.com/financial-aid/scholarships/types.

WORK-STUDY

The U.S. federal work-study program provides part-time jobs for undergraduate and graduate students with financial need so that they can earn money to pay for educational expenses. The focus of such work is on community service work and work related to a student's course of study. Not all schools participate in this program, so be sure to check with the school's financial aid office if this is something you are counting on. The sooner you apply, the more likely you are to get the job you desire and be able to benefit from the program, as funds are limited. For more information about this opportunity, visit https://studentaid .ed.gov/sa/types/work-study.

LOANS

Many types of loans are available. However, the important thing to remember here is that loans *must be paid back, with interest.* Be sure you understand the interest rate you will be charged. This is the extra cost of borrowing the money and is usually a percentage of the amount you borrow. Is this fixed, or will it change throughout time? Are the loan and interest deferred until you graduate (meaning you don't have to begin paying it off until after you graduate)? Is the loan subsidized (meaning the federal government pays the interest until you graduate)? These are all points you need to be clear about before you sign on the dotted line.

There are many types of loans offered to students, including need-based loans, non–need-based loans, state loans, and private loans. Two reputable federal loans are the Perkins Loan and the Direct Stafford Loan. For more information about student loans, start at https://bigfuture.collegeboard.org /pay-for-college/loans/types-of-college-loans.

FINANCIAL AID TIPS

- Some colleges and universities will offer tuition discounts to encourage students to attend, so tuition costs can be lower than they look at first.
- Apply for financial aid during your senior year of high school. The sooner you apply, the better your chances.
- Compare offers from different schools. One school may be able to match or improve on another school's financial aid offer.
- Keep your grades up. A good GPA helps a lot when it comes to merit scholarships and grants.

- You have to reapply for financial aid every year, so you'll be filling out that FAFSA form again.
- Look for ways that loans might be deferred or forgiven. Service commitment programs are a way to use service to pay back loans.

While You're in College

Once you're in an undergraduate program, you'll be taking all the classes required by your major. This will be time consuming and a lot of hard work, as it should be. But there's more to your college experience than that.

One of the great advantages of college is that it's so much more than simply training for a particular career. It's your opportunity to become a broader, deeper person. Use your electives to take courses far outside your major. Join clubs, intramural teams, improvisation groups—whatever catches your interest. Take a foreign language. The broader your worldview is, the more interesting you are as a person and the more appealing you are to employers in the future.

Working While You Learn

Your classes won't always convey what it's like to do the work in real life, especially in the constantly changing world of digital communications. If you have the opportunity, consider some of these ways to learn and work at the same time.

COOPERATIVE EDUCATION PROGRAMS

Cooperative education (co-op) programs are a structured way to alternate classroom instruction with on-the-job experience. There are co-op programs for all kinds of jobs. Co-op programs are run by the educational institution in partnership with several employers. Students usually alternate semesters in school with semesters at work.

A co-op program is not an internship. Students in co-op jobs typically work 40 hours a week during their work semesters and are paid a regular salary.

Participating in a co-op program means it will take longer to graduate, but you come out of school with a lot of legitimate work experience.

Be sure the college you attend is truly committed to its co-op program. Some are deeply committed to the idea of co-ops as integral to education, but others treat it more like an add-on program. Also, the company you co-op with is not obligated to hire you at the end of the program, but it can still be an excellent source of good references for you in your job search.

INTERNSHIPS

Internships are another way to gain work experience while you're in school. Internships are offered by employers and usually last one semester or one summer. You might work part-time or full-time, but you're usually paid in experience and college credit rather than money. There are paid internships in some fields, but they aren't common.

Making High School Count

If you are still in high school, there are many things you can do now to nurture your interest in digital communications and set yourself up for success. Consider these tips for your remaining years:

- Work on listening well and speaking and communicating clearly. Work on writing clearly and effectively.
- Learn how to learn. This means keeping an open mind, asking questions, asking for help when you need it, taking good notes, and doing your homework.
- Plan a daily homework schedule and keep up with it. Have a consistent, quiet place to study.
- Talk about your career interests with friends, family, and counselors. They may have connections to people in your community whom you can shadow or who will mentor you.
- Try new interests or activities, especially during your first two years of high school.

- Be involved in extracurricular activities that truly interest you and that say something about who you are and want to be.

Kids are under so much pressure these days to "do it all," but you should think about working smarter rather than harder. If you are involved in things you enjoy, your educational load won't seem like such a burden. Be sure to take time for self-care, such as sleep, unscheduled downtime, and other activities that you find fun and energizing. See chapter 4 for more ways to relieve and avoid stress.

Remember to take care of yourself and enjoy the journey to adulthood. *AntonioGuillem/iStock/Getty Images*

Summary

This chapter dove right in and talked about all the aspects of college and postsecondary schooling that you'll want to consider as you move forward. Remember that finding the right fit is especially important, as it increases the chances that you'll stay in school and finish your degree or program as well as have an amazing experience while you're there.

In this chapter, you learned a little about the kinds of degrees that you could pursue if you want a career in digital communications. You also learned about how to get the best education for the best deal. You learned a little about scholarships and financial aid, how the SAT and ACT tests work, how to write a unique personal statement that eloquently expresses your passions, and how to do your best at essays and other application requirements.

Use this chapter as a jumping-off point to dig deeper into your particular area of interest. Here are some tidbits of wisdom to leave you with:

- If you need to, take the SAT and ACT tests early in your junior year so you have time to take them again. Most schools automatically accept the highest scores (but be sure to check your specific schools' policies).
- Don't underestimate how important school visits are, especially when you're trying to find the right academic fit. Come prepared to ask questions that are not addressed on the school's website or in the literature.
- Your personal statements and essays are very important pieces of your application that can set you apart from others. Take the time and energy needed to make them unique and compelling.
- Don't assume you can't afford a school based on the "sticker price." Many schools offer great scholarships and aid to qualified students. It doesn't hurt to apply. This advice applies especially to minorities, veterans, and students with disabilities.
- Don't lose sight of the fact that it's important to pursue a career that you enjoy, are good at, and are passionate about. You'll be a happier person if you do so.

It has always seemed strange to me that in our endless discussions about education so little stress is laid on the pleasure of becoming an educated person, the enormous interest it adds to life. To be able to be caught up into the world of thought, that is to be educated.—Edith Hamilton[14]

At this point, your career goals and aspirations should be gelling. At the least, you should have a plan for finding out more information. And don't forget about networking, which was covered in more detail in chapter 2. Remember to do the research about the school or degree program before you reach out and especially before you visit. Faculty and staff find students who ask challenging questions much more impressive than those who ask questions that can be answered by spending 10 minutes on the school's website.

In chapter 4, we go into detail about the next steps—writing a résumé and cover letter, interviewing well, follow-up communications, and more. This is information you can use to secure internships, volunteer positions, summer jobs, and more. It's not only for college graduates. In fact, the sooner you can hone these communication skills, the better off you'll be in the professional world regardless of your job.

Writing Your Résumé and Interviewing

No matter what you aspire to be, having a well-written résumé and impeccable interviewing skills will help you reach your ultimate goals. This chapter provides some helpful tips and advice to build the best résumé and cover letter, how to interview well with all your prospective employers, and how to communicate effectively and professionally at all times. All the advice in this chapter isn't just for people entering the workforce full-time either. It can help you score that internship or summer job or help you give a great college interview to impress the admissions office.

After we talk about writing your résumé, the chapter discusses important interviewing skills that you can build and develop over time. The chapter also has some tips for dealing successfully with stress, which is an inevitable by-product of a busy life. Let's dive in!

Welcome to your new career. *Chris Ryan/iStock/Getty Images*

Finding and Applying for the Job

To apply for a job, you first have to know where to look for one. One of the quickest ways to find out what jobs are available in your field is to search the internet with whichever search engine you like best.

Online Job Sites

When companies want to hire new employees, they post job descriptions on job hunting or employee recruitment websites. These are a fantastic resource for you long before you're ready to actually apply for a job. You can read real job descriptions for real jobs and see what qualifications and experience are needed for the kinds of job you're interested in. You'll also get a good idea of the range of salaries and benefits that go with different types of digital communications professions.

Pay attention to the "Required Qualifications," of course, but also pay attention to the "Desired Qualifications"—these are the ones you don't have to have, but if you have them, you'll have an edge over other potential applicants.

Here are a few sites to get you started:

- www.monster.com
- www.indeed.com
- www.ziprecruiter.com
- www.glassdoor.com
- www.simplyhired.com

Professional Organizations

One of the services provided by most professional organizations is a list of open positions. Employers post jobs here because organization members are often the most qualified and experienced. The "Further Resources" section in this book lists professional organizations for the different digital communications professions we've covered. For other professions, check online and talk to people in your field (such as your professors) to find out which organizations to join and where the best source of job information is likely to be.

Networking

Some say the best way to find a job is through networking. Your personal and professional contacts may know about an upcoming job that hasn't even been advertised yet. Sometimes, an employer may even create a position for someone they want to hire. Keep in touch with the people you know in the field, at every level, and let them know that you're available.

> **Tip:** If you know someone who already works at the company or organization, ask him or her for some inside advice and find out whether it's okay to mention his or her name during the interview. If the interviewer finds out you know someone who works there, that can really work in your favor.

Still wondering about how to network? Flip back to the end of chapter 2 to the section devoted to networking for some useful tips.

Writing Your Résumé

If you're a teen writing a résumé for your first job, you likely don't have a lot of work experience under your belt yet. Because of this limited work experience, you need to include classes and course work that are related to the job you're seeking, any school activities and volunteer experience you have, and your best sample work. While you are writing your résumé, you might discover some talents and recall some activities you did that you forgot about but that are still important to add. Think about volunteer work, side jobs you've held, organizations you've been a member of, and the like.

NAME SURNAME

PROFESSION

CONTACTS

☐ +123.456.7890

🏠 123456, Address, City, State

✉ youremail@mail.com

🌐 www.yourweb.com

SKILLS

Skill #1

Skill #2

Skill #3

Skill #4

Skill #5

SOFTWARE

Software #1

Software #2

Software #3

Software #4

LANGUAGES

English ●●●●●●●●●●

French ●●●●●●●●○○

Chinese ●●●○○○○○○○

INTERESTS

📷 Lorem ipsum dolor sit amet, consectetur adipiscing elit. Pellentesque ac dolor sit amet quam fermentum tempus.

✈ Lorem ipsum dolor sit amet, consectetur adipiscing elit. Pellentesque ac dolor sit amet quam fermentum tempus.

⚽ Lorem ipsum dolor sit amet, consectetur adipiscing elit. Pellentesque ac dolor sit amet quam fermentum tempus.

PROFESSIONAL PROFILE

Lorem ipsum dolor sit amet, consectetur adipiscing elit. Pellentesque ac dolor sit amet quam fermentum tempus. Fusce ullamcorper gravida consequat. Phasellus mollis interdum lacus, vitae fermentum est luctus quis. In sed quam ac neque ornare egestas. Maecenas efficitur imperdiet sem in maximus. Fusce vitae augue ullamcorper, elementum velit sed, aliquam metus. Donec ut mollis orci. Etiam enim eros, tristique interdum malesuada non, tincidunt et sapien. Nunc sodales ante nec mi volutpat varius. Ut ac eros vel arcu efficitur blandit vel et leo. Cras in rhoncus dolor. Praesent pulvinar velit sed diam laoreet condimentum. Vestibulum scelerisque lorem non nibh faucibus condimentum. Suspendisse vel magna malesuada, scelerisque sapien sit amet, sodales orci.

Quisque convallis auctor libero eget vehicula. Suspendisse nisi turpis, convallis nec nulla ac, bibendum sodales tortor. Duis et velit nunc. Nulla ullamcorper augue eu odio accumsan posuere vel vel metus. Nam ac velit lacinia, molestie justo a, luctus purus. Aenean pellentesque nunc at elit volutpat aliquet. Suspendisse potenti. Pellentesque habitant morbi tristique senectus et netus et malesuada fames ac turpis egestas. Phasellus quis vehicula dolor, non aliquet ipsum. Ut mauris mauris, finibus non mattis vitae, pulvinar ornare ante. Sed nec porta elit.

EDUCATION

🎓 **2001-2005 DEGREE / MAJOR**
University / School Name

Lorem ipsum dolor sit amet, consectetur adipiscing elit. Pellentesque ac dolor sit amet quam fermentum tempus. Fusce ullamcorper gravida consequat. Phasellus mollis interdum lacus, vitae fermentum est luctus quis. In sed quam ac neque ornare egestas.

🎓 **2006-2010 DEGREE / MAJOR**
University / School Name

Lorem ipsum dolor sit amet, consectetur adipiscing elit. Pellentesque ac dolor sit amet quam fermentum tempus. Fusce ullamcorper gravida consequat. Phasellus mollis interdum lacus, vitae fermentum est luctus quis. In sed quam ac neque ornare egestas.

WORK EXPERIENCE

💼 **2018 -Present COMPANY NAME / POSITION**

Lorem ipsum dolor sit amet, consectetur adipiscing elit. Pellentesque ac dolor sit amet quam fermentum tempus. Fusce ullamcorper gravida consequat. Phasellus mollis interdum lacus, vitae fermentum est luctus quis. In sed quam ac neque ornare egestas. Maecenas efficitur imperdiet sem in maximus. Fusce vitae augue ullamcorper, elementum velit sed, aliquam metus.

💼 **2018 -2015 COMPANY NAME / POSITION**

Lorem ipsum dolor sit amet, consectetur adipiscing elit. Pellentesque ac dolor sit amet quam fermentum tempus. Fusce ullamcorper gravida consequat. Phasellus mollis interdum lacus, vitae fermentum est luctus quis. In sed quam ac neque ornare egestas. Maecenas efficitur imperdiet sem in maximus. Fusce vitae augue ullamcorper, elementum velit sed, aliquam metus.

💼 **2018 -2015 COMPANY NAME / POSITION**

Lorem ipsum dolor sit amet, consectetur adipiscing elit. Pellentesque ac dolor sit amet quam fermentum tempus. Fusce ullamcorper gravida consequat. Phasellus mollis interdum lacus, vitae fermentum est luctus quis. In sed quam ac neque ornare egestas. Maecenas efficitur imperdiet sem in maximus. Fusce vitae augue ullamcorper, elementum velit sed, aliquam metus.

ACHIEVEMENTS

🏅 **2015 ACHIEVEMENT #1**
Lorem ipsum dolor sit amet, consectetur adipiscing elit. Pellentesque ac dolor sit amet quam fermentum tempus.

🏅 **2017 ACHIEVEMENT #2**
Lorem ipsum dolor sit amet, consectetur adipiscing elit. Pellentesque ac dolor sit amet quam fermentum tempus.

REFERENCES

Reference Name	**Reference Name**	**Reference Name**
Position title	Position title	Position title
referencename@mail.com	referencename@mail.com	referencename@mail.com
+123.456.7890	+123.456.7890	+123.456.7890

As someone in a creative field, your résumé should be visually unique and compelling. *Vera Fedorova/iStock/Getty Images*

PARTS OF A RÉSUMÉ

As mentioned, the functional résumé is the best approach when you don't have a lot of pertinent work experience, as it is written to highlight your abilities rather than the experience. The other, perhaps more common type of résumé is called the chronological résumé, and it lists a person's accomplishments in chronological order, the most recent jobs being listed first. This section breaks down and discusses the functional résumé in greater detail.

Here are some typical parts of a résumé:

- **Heading:** This should include your name, address, and contact information, including phone, e-mail, and portfolio website if you have one.
- **Education:** Always list your most recent school or program first. Include date of completion (or expected date of graduation), degree or certificate earned, and the institution's name and address. Include workshops, seminars, and related classes here as well.
- **Skills:** Skills include computer literacy, leadership skills, organizational skills, or time management skills. Be specific in this area when possible.
- **Activities:** These can be related to skills. Perhaps an activity listed here led to you developing a skill listed above. This section can be combined with the "Skills" section, but it's often helpful to break these apart if you have enough substantive things to say in both areas. Examples include leadership roles, community service work, clubs, and organizations.
- **Experience:** If you don't have any actual work experience that's relevant, you might consider skipping this section. However, you can list digital communications projects if you have relevant work to show.
- **Interests:** This section is optional, but it's a chance to include special talents and interests. Keep it short, factual, and specific.
- **Languages:** List all the scripting and programming languages you've used as well as relevant software, such as Photoshop, Acrobat, InDesign, and so on.
- **References:** It's best to say that references are available on request. If you do list actual contacts, list no more than three and make sure you inform your contacts that they might be contacted.

The "Skills," "Interests," "Experience," and "Languages" entries can be creatively combined or developed to maximize your abilities and experience. These are not set-in-stone sections that every résumé must have.

If you're still not seeing the big picture here, it's helpful to look at résumé and portfolio examples online to see how others have approached this process. Search for "digital communications résumé examples" or "example portfolios" to get a look at some examples.

RÉSUMÉ-WRITING TIPS

Regardless of your situation and why you're writing the résumé, here are some basic tips and techniques you should use:

- Keep it short, attractive, and compelling. Your design can be unique and clever but make sure it doesn't get in the way of readability.
- Use simple language. Keep it to one page.
- Highlight your academic achievements, such as a high grade-point average (above 3.5) or academic awards. If you have taken classes related to the job you're interviewing for, list those briefly as well.
- Emphasize your extracurricular activities, internships, and so on. Use these activities to show your skills, interests, and abilities.
- Use action verbs, such as "led," "designed," "created," "taught," "ran," and "developed."
- Be specific and give examples.
- Always be honest.
- Include leadership roles and experience.
- Edit and proofread at least twice and have someone else do the same. Ask a professional (such as your school writing center or your local library services) to proofread it for you also. Don't forget to run the spell-checker.
- In some cases, include a cover letter (discussed next).

The Cover Letter

Every résumé you send out via the standard mail should include a cover letter. This can be the most important part of your job search because it's often the first thing that potential employers read. By including the cover letter, you're showing the school or organization that you took the time to learn about them and address them personally. This goes a long way to show that you're interested in the position.

Be sure to call the organization or verify on the website the name and title of the person to whom you should address the letter. This letter should be brief. Introduce yourself and begin with a statement that will grab the person's attention. Keep in mind that they will potentially be receiving hundreds of résumés and cover letters for an open position. You want yours to stand out. Important information to include in the cover letter, from the top, includes the following:

- The current date
- Your address and contact information
- The person's name, company's name, and contact information

Then you begin the letter portion of the cover letter, which should mention how you heard about the position, something extra about you that will interest the potential employer, practical skills you can bring to the position, and past experience related to the job. You should apply the facts outlined in your résumé to the job to which you're applying. Each cover letter should be personalized for the position or company to which you're applying. Don't use "to whom it may concern." Instead, take the time to find out to whom you should actually address the letter. Finally, end with a closing, such as "Sincerely, Piper E. Smith," and be sure to add your signature. Search for "sample cover letters for internships" or "sample cover letters for high schoolers" to see some good examples.

When you are e-mailing your résumé, you'll need to pay particular attention to the subject line of your e-mail. Be sure that it is specific to the position you are applying for. In fact, you should follow all the guidelines discussed in the above paragraphs for creating a cover letter when you write your introductory e-mail.

In all cases, it's really important to follow the employer's instructions on how to submit your cover letter and résumé. Generally, sending PDF documents rather than, for example, editable Word documents is a better idea, as everyone can read a PDF but might not be able to read the version of Word that you used. Most word processing programs have an option under the Save command that allows you to save your work as a PDF.

LINKING IN WITH IMPACT

In addition to your paper or electronic résumé, creating a LinkedIn profile is a good way to highlight your experience and promote yourself as well as to network. Joining professional organizations or connecting with other people in your desired field is a good way to keep abreast of changes and trends and work opportunities.

The key elements of a LinkedIn profile are your photo, your headline, and your profile summary. These are the most revealing parts of the profile and the ones that employers and connections will base their impression of you on.

The photo should be carefully chosen. Remember that LinkedIn is not Facebook or Instagram: it is not the place to share a photo of you acting too casually on vacation or at a party. According to Joshua Waldman, author of *Job Searching with Social Media for Dummies*,[1] the choice of photo should be taken seriously and be done right. His tips are as follows:

- Choose a photo in which you have a nice smile.
- Dress in professional clothing.
- Ensure that the background of the photo is pleasing to the eye. According to Waldman, some colors—like green and blue—convey a feeling of trust and stability.
- Remember that it's not a mug shot. You can be creative with the angle of your photo rather than stare directly into the camera.
- Use your photo to convey some aspect of your personality.
- Focus on your face. Remember that visitors to your profile will see only a small thumbnail image, so be sure your face takes up most of it.

Interviewing Skills

The best way to avoid nerves and keep calm when you're interviewing is to be prepared. It's okay to feel scared but keep it in perspective. It's likely that you'll receive many more rejections in your professional life than acceptances (as we all do). However, you need only one "yes" to start out.

Think of the interviewing process as a learning experience. With the right attitude, you will learn from each experience and get better with each subsequent interview. That should be your overarching goal. Consider these tips and tricks when interviewing, whether it be for an actual job, internship, college admission, or something else entirely:[2]

- Practice interviewing with a friend or relative. Practicing will help calm your nerves and make you feel more prepared. Ask for specific feedback from your friends. Do you need to speak louder? Are you making enough eye contact? Are you actively listening when the other person is speaking?
- Learn as much as you can about the company or organization. Also be sure to understand the position for which you're applying. This will show the interviewer that you are motivated and interested in the organization.
- Speak up during the interview. Convey to the interviewer important points about you. Don't be afraid to ask questions. Try to remember the interviewer's name and call him or her by name. Consider these questions:
  - What created the need to fill this position? Is it a new position, or has someone left the company?
  - Where does this position fit in the overall hierarchy of the organization?
  - What are the key skills required to succeed in this job?
  - What challenges might I expect to face within the first six months on the job?
  - How does this position relate to the achievement of the company's (or department's or boss's) goals?
  - How would you describe the company culture?
- Arrive early and dress professionally and appropriately (you can read more about proper dress in a following section).
- Take some time to prepare answers to commonly asked questions. Be ready to describe your career or educational goals to the interviewer.

Common questions you may be asked during a job interview include the following:

- Tell me about yourself.
- What are your greatest strengths?
- What are your weaknesses?
- Tell me something about yourself that's not on your résumé.
- What are your career goals?
- How do you handle failure? Are you willing to fail?
- How do you handle stress and pressure?
- What are you passionate about?
- Why do you want to work for us?

Common questions you may be asked during a college admissions interview include the following:

- Tell me about yourself.
- Why are you interested in going to college?
- Why do you want to major in this subject?
- What are your academic strengths?
- What are your academic weaknesses? How have you addressed them?
- What will you contribute to this college/school/university?
- Where do you see yourself in 10 years?
- How do you handle failure? Are you willing to fail?
- How do you handle stress and pressure?
- Whom do you most admire?
- What is your favorite book?
- What do you do for fun?
- Why are you interested in this college/school/university?

Jot down notes about your answers to these questions but don't try to memorize the answers. You don't want to come off too rehearsed during the interview. Remember to be as specific and detailed as possible when answering these questions. Your goal is to set yourself apart in some way from the other people they will interview. Always accentuate the positive, even when you're asked about something you did not like or about failure or stress. Most important, be yourself.

Note: *Active listening* is the process of fully concentrating on what is being said, understanding it, and providing nonverbal cues and responses to the person talking.[3] It's the opposite of being distracted and thinking about something else when someone is talking. Active listening takes practice. You might find that your mind wanders and you need to bring it back to the person talking (this could happen multiple times during one conversation). Practice this technique in regular conversations with friends and relatives. In addition to giving a better interview, it can cut down on nerves and make you more popular with friends and family, as everyone wants to feel that they are really being heard. For more on active listening, check out www.mindtools.com/CommSkll/ActiveListening.htm.

As mentioned, you should also be ready to ask questions of your interviewer. In a practical sense, there should be some questions that you have that you can't find the answer to on the website or in the literature. Also, asking questions shows that you are interested and have done your homework. Avoid asking questions about salary/scholarships or special benefits at this stage and don't ask about anything negative that you've heard about the company. Keep the questions positive and relative to you and the position to which you're applying. Some example questions to potential employers include the following:

- What is a typical career path for a person in this position?
- How would you describe the ideal candidate for this position?
- How is the department organized?
- What kind of responsibilities come with this job? (Don't ask this if they've already addressed this question in the job description or discussion.)
- What can I do as a follow-up?
- When do you expect to reach a decision?

See the sidebar "Make the Most of School Visits" in chapter 3 for some good example questions to ask the college admissions office. The important thing is to write your own questions related to answers you really want to know. This will show genuine interest. Be sure your question isn't answered on the website, in the job description, or in the literature.

TO SHAKE OR NOT TO SHAKE?

Shaking hands in the twenty-first century is something to think about. *PeopleImages/ iStock/Getty Images*

A handshake is a traditional form of greeting, especially in business. When you arrive for a job interview—or just meet someone new—a firm handshake shows that you are a person to be taken seriously.

But shaking hands is not done in every culture, and even in North America, the norm of shaking hands has changed. During the COVID-19 crisis, people stopped shaking hands to avoid spreading germs. As things get back to normal, some people will want to resume shaking hands, and some people won't.

When you arrive for a job interview, follow the lead of the person you're meeting with. A respectful head nod is just fine.

Dressing Appropriately

It's important to determine what is actually appropriate in the setting of the interview. What is appropriate in a large corporate setting might be different from what you'd expect at a small liberal arts college or at a creative design firm. Most college admissions offices suggest "business casual" dress, for example, but depending on the job interview, you may want to step it up from there.

Again, it's important to do your homework and come prepared. In addition to reading up on their guidelines, it never hurts to take a look around the company's or school's website if you can to see what other people are wearing to work or to interviews.

In general, business casual means less formal than business attire, like a suit but a step up from jeans, T-shirt, and sneakers:

- **For men:** You can't go wrong with khaki pants, a polo or button-up shirt, and brown or black shoes.
- **For women:** Nice slacks, a shirt or blouse that isn't too revealing, and nice flats or shoes with a heel that's not too high will work.

Tip: You may want to find out in advance whether the organization has a dress code. Don't hesitate to ask the person who's going to interview you if you're unsure what to wear. You can also call the main number and ask the receptionist what people typically wear to interviews.

Regardless of the setting, make sure your clothes are not wrinkled, untidy, or stained. Avoid clothing of any kind that is revealing.

Even something like "business casual" can be interpreted in many ways, so do some research to find out what exactly is expected of you. *seb_ra/iStock/Getty Images*

Follow-Up Communication

Be sure to follow up, whether by e-mail or regular mail, with a thank-you note to the interviewer. This is true whether you're interviewing for a job or interviewing with a college. A handwritten thank-you note, posted in the regular mail, is best. In addition to being considerate, it will trigger the interviewer's memory about you, and it shows that you have genuine interest in the position, company, or school. Be sure to follow the business-letter format and highlight the key points of your interview and experience at the company/university. Be prompt with your thank-you. Put it in the mail the day after your interview (or send the e-mail the same day).

EFFECTIVELY HANDLING STRESS

As you're forging ahead with your life plans, whether it's college, a full-time job, or even a gap year, you might find that these decisions feel very important and heavy and that the stress is difficult to deal with. That's completely normal. Try these simple stress-relieving techniques:

- Take deep breaths in and out. Try this for 30 seconds. You'll be amazed at how it can help.
- Close your eyes and clear your mind.
- Go scream at the passing subway car, lock yourself in a closet and scream, or scream into a pillow. For some people, this can really help.
- Keep the issue in perspective. Any decision you make now can be changed if it doesn't work out.

Want ways to avoid stress altogether? They are surprisingly simple. Of course, simple doesn't always mean easy, but it means they are basic and make sense with what we know about the human body:

- Get enough sleep.
- Eat healthy.
- Get exercise.

- Go outside.
- Schedule downtime.
- Connect with friends and family.

The bottom line is that you need to take time for self-care. There will always be conflict, but how you deal with it makes all the difference. This only becomes more important as you enter college or the workforce and maybe have a family. Developing good, consistent habits related to self-care now will serve you all your life.

What Employers Expect

Regardless of the job, profession, or field, there are universal characteristics that all employers (and schools for that matter) look for in potential employees. At this early stage in your professional life, you have an opportunity to recognize which of these foundational characteristics are your strengths (and therefore highlight them in an interview) and which are weaknesses (and therefore continue to work on them and build them up). Consider the following universal characteristics that all employers look for:

- Positive attitude
- Dependability
- Desire to continue to learn
- Initiative
- Effective communication
- Cooperation
- Organization
- Passion for the profession

This is not an exhaustive list, and other characteristics may include things like being creative, being sensitive to others, being honest, having good judgment, being loyal, being responsible, and being on time. Consider these important characteristics when you answer the common questions that employers ask. It pays to work these traits into the answers while being honest and realistic about yourself.

BEWARE WHAT YOU SHARE ON SOCIAL MEDIA

Most of us engage in social media. Sites such as Facebook, Twitter, and Instagram provide us a platform for sharing photos and memories, opinions, and life events and reveal everything from our political stance to our sense of humor. It's a great way to connect with people around the world, but once you post something, it's accessible to anyone—including potential employers—unless you take mindful precautions.

Your posts may be public, which means you may be making the wrong impression without realizing it. More and more, people are using search engines like Google to get a sense of potential employers, colleagues, or employees, and the impression you make online can have a strong impact on how you are perceived. According to CareerBuilder.com,[4] 60 percent of employers search for information on candidates on social media sites.

Glassdoor.com[5] offers the following tips for how to avoid your social media activity from sabotaging your career success:

1. Check your privacy settings. Ensure that your photos and posts are accessible only to the friends or contacts you want to see them. You want to come across as professional and reliable.
2. Rather than avoiding social media while searching for a job, use it to your advantage. Give future employees a sense of your professional interest by "liking" pages or joining groups of professional organizations related to your career goals.
3. Grammar counts. Be attentive to the quality of writing of all your posts and comments.
4. Be consistent. With each social media outlet, there is a different focus and tone of what you are communicating. LinkedIn is very professional, while Facebook is far more social and relaxed. It's okay to take a different tone on various social media sites but be sure you aren't blatantly contradicting yourself.
5. Choose your user name carefully. Remember, social media may be the first impression anyone has of you in the professional realm.

MICHAEL RUBINO, EDITOR IN CHIEF
AT *INDIANAPOLIS MONTHLY*

Michael Rubino. *Courtesy of Michael Rubino*

Michael Rubino graduated from Wabash College with a degree in English and received his master's degree in journalism from Indiana University. His first job was working as a sportswriter for a newspaper on the cusp of the digital area. He spent 10 years in the newspaper field, mostly in sportswriting. His work has appeared in the *New York Times*, the *Christian Science Monitor*, and ESPN.com and has been noted by the *Best American Sports Writing* anthologies. He has been the editor in chief of the *Indianapolis Monthly* magazine since 2016.

Can you explain how you ended up in the digital field? What about it interested you?

During my first time at *Indianapolis Monthly*, around 2009, I was immersed in learning how to write a magazine story, which is a longer-form style. I had been at various newspapers before that. I was a fan of social media, and I saw the power of it, but I wondered how I could incorporate it into my job on a daily basis.

When I got laid off, I realized I needed to be my own brand. I had to stand for something—to have an expertise in an area. I needed to build a name for myself and do a certain kind of story. I did that through social media and digital. It helped my career immensely. It expanded my audience and showed me other ideas and other writers. It don't think I would have had the opportunity to come back to the magazine if not for that. When I came back in 2014, I was much more interested in the digital aspect as a media outlet and am still heavily involved in that today. I love the print product and always will, but the potential for digital is much larger.

What's a "typical" day in your job?

I get in to the office about 8:00 a.m. Before that, I consume an hour or so of media (TV, Twitter, etcetera), so that I'm going into work with a head full of what is to come.

At about 8:30, the editor and I have a planning meeting/status check. We discuss stories to pursue, social media strategy, potential podcast guests, website issues, etcetera. We close that meeting with marching orders. We also discuss long-term podcast ideas—I help hash them out with the editor. We talk about formatting issues, the value of what we are giving, whether it's working, and so on. Throughout the day, I have other mid- to long-term planning meetings.

We are small, so every day is different. The weeks tend to be generally the same—two weeks are planning and writing, and the other two weeks involve hardcore production and editing as well as printing the print product.

Overall, my immediate tasks deal with digital issues and guiding our digital offerings. Digital issues, such as e-mail lists, podcast topics, web-only stories, etcetera, are a big chunk of my day. It's about putting out fires and solving problems. I spend at least half of my time on digital issues, maybe more.

What's the greatest challenge the digital market faces at this time? What are your greatest challenges, day in and day out?

So, I used to teach at the university level, and students so often wanted to do cool stuff with technology. That's great except when they weren't as concerned with telling good stories. The technology will change, but being a good storyteller won't. You have to be able to tell a story well no matter what technology you're using. You can tell a story in any medium.

My challenge is, when there is a new technology, I have to learn it quickly, and the learning curve is often steep. That process can slow me down and overwhelm me sometimes. For example, if we want to do a podcast, our small staff has to figure out how all that works. We can't usually freelance that out. I have to learn all the ins and outs, and I feel like I'm playing catch-up constantly. If you don't keep up, you will quickly become irrelevant. The speed that technology changes is staggering.

For example, many media outlets are trying to do something with TikTok. Should we use it as a city magazine? We don't have the budget to outsource this, and we want to do it well if we are going to do it.

The issue is the multitude of delivery mechanisms for stories—and our question comes down to which ones can we learn quickly enough so we can offer something that's cool and engaging. Some we just can't do. We do want to expand our base but also continue to attract our key audience.

What's the best part of being in the digital market?

I really enjoy connecting with people on a level that's not possible in a monthly print magazine. You can reach people and share a story on a mass scale. These stories feel personal once you've spent time researching and writing them. You get invested, so it's especially cool to reach people all over the country and get so much immediate feedback. That is so cool, gratifying, and humbling. It's a concentrated dose of print, totally sped up.

Stories written for Indianapolis readers can appeal to people across the country. When a story is online, many more people respond via e-mail or social media (immediately), and the audience is many multiples of the size of our subscription holders. This magnifies and multiplies the responses you get. When you have a story that goes viral online, it's so exciting and frightening—sheer terror and ecstasy all at once. It's amazing. The responses can be amazing and overwhelming. The reach and power of the digital world is humbling and exciting.

Do you think your education adequately prepared you for your current job?

I do because I learned at college how to be a critical thinker and how to write well. Wabash College gave me a great education. Although I also learned a lot at IU when getting my master's in journalism, I wouldn't be anywhere without my Wabash College education.

Where do you see this field going in the future?

It will continue to become fractured. The digital revolution has fractured media to where it's a series of specialized areas. All media is now the thing that you are obsessed with. Podcasts etcetera—they are all about very specific topics that are niche and fractured. That's what technology has done to media. I think more of the same for the future—more stuff like specialized, serialized podcasts on whatever issue you want to hear about. The goal is to try to reach people where they are, but people switch where they are very quickly.

But the core stays the same—if you know how to tell a good story, you'll find an audience. That will never change. The technology and applications will always change.

What advice do you have for young people considering this career?

A broad-based liberal arts education prepares you well for any field. I go back to the basics, and they do not change. How you communicate will change—*what* you communicate won't change.

Telling stories is what it's about. Hone your writing skills and get a general liberal arts education. Knowing the fundamentals of communication is important. Become the best communicator you can and be open to the technology of the day. You do need the know-how to tell the stories.

How can a young person prepare for this career while in high school?
Talk with as many people as you can in the industry. But remember that no one person has the magic answer because that doesn't exist. Do your due diligence and learn from others, take it all in, think about what they say, but know that there isn't just one right way to do something. If you believe in an idea, you should go ahead and do it. There is no one right way to do digital. There is no secret to life.

===

Note: *Personal contacts can make the difference.* Don't be afraid to contact designers and multimedia artists and other professionals you know. Personal connections can be a great way to find jobs and internship opportunities. Your high school teachers, your coaches and mentors, and your friends' parents are all examples of people who very well may know about jobs or opportunities that would suit you. Start asking several months before you hope to start a job or internship because it will take some time to do research and arrange interviews. You can also use social media in your search. LinkedIn, for example, includes lots of searchable information on local companies. Follow and interact with people on social media to get their attention. Just remember to act professionally and communicate with proper grammar just as you would in person.

Summary

Well, you made it to the end of this book. It is hoped that you have learned enough about the digital communications fields to start your journey or to continue with your path. If you've reached the end and you feel like some form of digital communications is your passion, that's great news. Or if you've figured out that it isn't the right field for you, that's good information to learn too. For many of us, figuring out what we *don't* want to do and what we don't like is an important step in finding the right career.

With passion, creativity, and hard work, you can be successful in the digital communications field.
PeopleImages/E+/Getty Images

> If you want to get into podcasting, you can learn a lot through self-education from YouTube and so on. Start by learning different technical areas of websites. Learn how businesses are using social media to promote their websites. Learn the principles of marketing—digital marketing and general. Be sure to listen to podcasts that you like. Listen to all different types of podcasts, and you'll learn what works and what is good about different types of shows. Figure out the audience.—Lauren Wrighton, podcast manager and producer

There is a lot of good news about the digital communications fields. They are great career choices for anyone with a passion for communication. It's also a great career for people who get energy from working in creative settings. Job demand is good and growing. Having a plan and an idea about your future can help guide your decisions. It is hoped that by reading this book, you are well on your way to having a plan for your future. Good luck to you as you move ahead.

Notes

Introduction

1. Bureau of Labor Statistics, "Public Relations Specialists—Summary," *Occupational Outlook Handbook*, updated April 9, 2021, accessed September 12, 2020, www.bls.gov/ooh/media-and-communication/public-relations-specialists.htm.

2. Bureau of Labor Statistics, "Advertising, Promotions, and Marketing Managers—Summary," *Occupational Outlook Handbook*, updated April 14, 2021, accessed September 12, 2020, www.bls.gov/ooh/management/advertising-promotions-and-marketing-managers.htm.

3. Bureau of Labor Statistics, "Market Research Analysts—Summary," *Occupational Outlook Handbook*, updated April 14, 2021, accessed September 12, 2020, www.bls.gov/ooh/business-and-financial/market-research-analysts.htm.

4. Elka Torpey, "You're a What? Social Media Specialist," *Career Outlook*, *Bureau of Labor Statistics*, November 2016, accessed September 12, 2020, www.bls.gov/careeroutlook/2016/youre-a-what/social-media-specialist.htm.

5. Matthew McLean, "Want to Work in Podcasting? Your Guide to Finding Podcasting Jobs," *Podcast Host*, July 19, 2018, accessed September 12, 2020, www.thepodcasthost.com/business-of-podcasting/get-a-podcast-job.

6. Bureau of Labor Statistics, "Graphic Designers: Job Outlook," *Occupational Outlook Handbook*, updated April 14, 2021, accessed September 12, 2020, www.bls.gov/ooh/arts-and-design/graphic-designers.htm#tab-6.

Chapter 1

1. Bureau of Labor Statistics, "How to Become a Graphic Designer," *Occupational Outlook Handbook*, updated April 9, 2021, accessed September 12, 2020, www.bls.gov/ooh/arts-and-design/graphic-designers.htm#tab-4.

2. "Digital Media Specialist Job Description," *Workable.com*, accessed September 12, 2020, https://resources.workable.com/digital-media-specialist-job-description.

3. "What Is a Digital Marketing Specialist?" *CareerExplorer*, accessed September 12, 2020, www.careerexplorer.com/careers/digital-marketing-specialist.

4. Elka Torpey, "You're a What? Social Media Specialist," *Career Outlook, Bureau of Labor Statistics*, November 2016, accessed September 12, 2020, www.bls.gov/careeroutlook /2016/youre-a-what/social-media-specialist.htm.

5. "Web Analytics Specialist," *CareerMatch*, accessed September 19, 2020, www .careermatch.com/job-prep/career-insights/profiles/web-analytics-specialist.

6. Aaron Dowd, "Podcasting with Aaron," *Podplay.com*, December 22, 2018, accessed September 19, 2020, www.podplay.com/en/podcast/157582/podcasting-with -aaron/episode/19939358/how-to-get-a-job-producing-podcasts.

7. Bureau of Labor Statistics, "Web Developers and Digital Designers—Summary," *Occupational Outlook Handbook*, updated April 9, 2021, accessed September 19, 2020, www.bls.gov/ooh/computer-and-information-technology/web-developers.htm.

8. Bureau of Labor Statistics, "Advertising, Promotions, and Marketing Managers—Summary," *Occupational Outlook Handbook*, updated April 14, 2021, accessed September 19, 2020, www.bls.gov/ooh/management/advertising-promotions -and-marketing-managers.htm.

9. Torpey, "You're a What? Social Media Specialist."

10. "SEO Specialist," *Study.com*, January 12, 2021, accessed September 19, 2020, https://study.com/articles/seo_specialist_job_description_salary_training.html.

11. "Podcasters—Work Environment," *Vault*, accessed September 19, 2020, www.vault.com/industries-professions/professions/p/podcasters/work-environment.

Chapter 2

1. Daniella Alscher, "How to Build a Graphic Design Portfolio for the Clueless Beginner," *Learn.g2.com*, March 28, 2019, accessed September 19, 2020, https://learn .g2.com/graphic-design-portfolio.

2. Bureau of Labor Statistics, "How to Become a Graphic Designer," *Occupational Outlook Handbook*, updated April 9, 2021, accessed September 19, 2020, www.bls.gov /ooh/arts-and-design/graphic-designers.htm#tab-4.

3. Mathew Hilton, "Leverage Your Volunteering Experience When Applying to Physical Therapy School," *CovalentCareers.com*, May 11, 2016, accessed September 19, 2020, https://covalent careers.com/resources/volunteer-experience -physical-therapy-school.

4. Lou Adler, "New Survey Reveals 85 Percent of All Jobs Are Filled via Networking," *LinkedIn.com*, February 29, 2016, accessed September 19, 2020, www .linkedin.com/pulse/new-survey-reveals -85-all-jobs-filled-via-networking-lou-adler.

Chapter 3

1. Gap Year Association, "Gap Year Data and Benefits," accessed September 12, 2020, www.gapyearassociation.org/data-benefits.php.

2. Isaac Asimov, *The Roving Mind* (Amherst, NY: Prometheus Books, 1983), 116.

3. Peter Van Buskirk, "Finding a Good College Fit," *U.S. News & World Report*, June 13, 2011, accessed September 19, 2020, www.usnews.com/education/blogs /the-college-admissions-insider/2011/06/13/finding-a-good-college-fit.

4. National Center for Education Statistics, "Fast Facts: Graduation Rates," accessed September 19, 2020, https://nces.ed.gov/fastfacts/display.asp?id=40.

5. U.S. Department of Education, "Focusing Higher Education on Student Success," July 27, 2015, accessed September 19, 2020, www.ed.gov/news/press-releases /fact-sheet-focusing-higher-education-student-success.

6. National Center for Education Statistics, "Digest for Education Statistics," November 2014, accessed September 19, 2020, https://nces.ed.gov/programs/digest /d14/tables/dt14_502.30.asp; U.S. Bureau of Labor Statistics, "Labor Force Statistics from the Current Population Survey," updated January 22, 2021, accessed September 19, 2020, www.bls.gov/cps/cpsaat07.htm.

7. U.S. Department of Education, "Six-Year Attainment, Persistence, Transfer, Retention, and Withdrawal Rates of Students Who Began Postsecondary Education in 2003–04," July 2011, accessed September 19, 2020, https://nces.ed.gov/pubs2011 /2011152.pdf.

8. "Create an Awesome Design Portfolio with These 20 Pro Tips," *Canva.com*, www.canva.com/learn/portfolio.

9. Allison Wignall, "Preference of the ACT or SAT by State (Infographic)," *CollegeRaptor*, November 14, 2019, accessed September 19, 2020, www.collegeraptor .com/getting-in/articles/act-sat/preference-act-sat-state-infographic.

10. Jennifer Ma, Sandy Baum, Matea Pender, and C. J. Libassi, *Trends in College Pricing 2019* (New York: College Board, 2019), accessed September 19, 2020, https:// research.collegeboard.org/trends/college-pricing/highlights.

11. "Focus on Net Price, Not Sticker Price," *College Board*, accessed September 19, 2020, https://bigfuture.collegeboard.org/pay-for-college/paying-your-share-focus-on -net-price-not-sticker-price.

12. "Trends in College Pricing and Student Aid 2020," *College Board*, accessed September 19, 2020, https://research.collegeboard.org/trends/college-pricing/figures-tables/average-net-price-sector-over-time.

13. "Learn What's New with the FAFSA Process," *U.S. Department of Education*, accessed December 14, 2020, https://financialaidtoolkit.ed.gov/tk/learn/fafsa/updates.jsp.

14. Edith Hamilton, quoted in the *Saturday Evening Post*, September 27, 1958.

Chapter 4

1. Joshua Waldman, *Job Searching with Social Media for Dummies*, 2nd ed. (Hoboken, NJ: John Wiley & Sons, 2013), 149.

2. Justin Ross Muchnick, *Teens' Guide to College and Career Planning*, 12th ed. (Lawrenceville, NJ: Peterson's Publishing, 2015), 179–80.

3. "Active Listening: Hear What People Are Really Saying," *Mind Tools*, accessed November 29, 2020, www.mindtools.com/CommSkll/ActiveListening.htm.

4. "Press Releases," *CareerBuilder.com*, accessed November 29, 2020, www.careerbuilder.com/share/aboutus/pressreleasesdetail.aspx?ed=12%2F31%2F2016&id=pr945&sd=4%2F28%2F2016.

5. "Nine Things to Avoid on Social Media While Looking for a New Job," *Glassdoor.com*, January 3, 2018, accessed December 14, 2020, www.glassdoor.com/blog/things-to-avoid-on-social-media-job-search.

Glossary

1. Wikipedia, s.v., "Podcast," last modified April 30, 2021, accessed December 14, 2020, https://en.wikipedia.org/wiki/Podcast.

2. Wikipedia, s.v., "Search Engine Optimization," last modified April 30, 2021, accessed December 14, 2020, https://en.wikipedia.org/wiki/Search_engine_optimization.

Glossary

2D animation: a type of animation in which the images are "flat," meaning they have width and height but no depth.

3D animation: a type of animation in which images appear in a three-dimensional space, with width, height, and depth.

accreditation: the act of officially recognizing an organizational body, person, or educational facility as having a particular status or being qualified to perform a particular activity. For example, schools and colleges are accredited. *See also* certification.

Acrobat: Adobe's document-management program that creates, edits, and manages documents in Portable Document Format (PDF), which means the document looks the same regardless of which operating system or hardware setup is used to view it.

Adobe suite of products: the industry standard applications for many graphic design jobs, creations, and positions. Includes Photoshop, Illustrator, Dreamweaver, Acrobat, and InDesign.

American College Test (ACT): one of the standardized college entrance tests that anyone wanting to enter undergraduate studies in the United States should take. It measures knowledge and skills in mathematics, English, reading, and science reasoning as they apply to college readiness. There are four multiple-choice sections. There is also an optional writing test. The total score of the ACT is 36. *See also* Scholastic Aptitude Test.

animation: the art of creating electronic images with a computer in order to create moving images.

artist/animator: the person who creates environments and other animated, interactive images for designs.

associate degree: a degree awarded by community or junior colleges that typically requires two years of study. However, this can vary by degree earned and by the university awarding the degree.

bachelor's degree: an undergraduate degree awarded by colleges and universities that's typically a four-year course of study when pursued full-time. However, this can vary by degree earned and by the university awarding the degree.

blogger: a person who produces content online for a blog, usually from his or her own perspective and based on a particular subject matter.

body of work: all of the pieces ever made by a single artist (sometimes called their "oeuvre").

broadcast journalist: a journalist who produces audiovisual content for radio, the internet, or television as opposed to print.

business model: a map for the successful creation and operation of a business, including sources of revenue, target customer base, products, and details of financing.

certification: the action or process of confirming certain skills or knowledge on a person. Usually provided by some third-party review, assessment, or educational body. Individuals, not organizations, are certified. *See also* accreditation.

content creation specialists: workers who create content strategies, research trending topics, and write content for online use. Those who thrive in this profession have great writing skills and a strong ability to market their work.

cover letter: a document that usually accompanies a résumé and allows a candidate applying to a job or a school or internship an opportunity to describe his or her motivation and qualifications.

creative: to have the ability to make something that did not previously exist; used in the business world to refer to a person who does creative work, such as graphic artists or web designers.

criticism: the discussion or evaluation of a creative work, usually in terms of its perceived quality.

critique: the process of describing and analyzing a creative work; in the class-room, critiques are a regular part of the learning process in which the teacher and other students give their responses to a particular piece and discuss its qualities, both positive and negative. It is a useful process for both those giving and those receiving the critique.

deadlines: targets set relating to when a particular task needs to be completed.

digital advertising and marketing professionals: workers who develop effective marketing campaigns online and translate business goals into successful marketing campaigns. Their goals usually include increasing brand awareness, promoting company products or services, and driving up sales.

digital images: a computer file consisting of picture elements called pixels. High-resolution digital images usually have at least 300 pixels per square inch at full size and are used for printed images. Low-resolution digital images usually have 72 pixels per square inch and are used online. Common digital image types are JPG, PNG, TIFF, GIF, and PostScript.

doctorate degree: the highest level of degree awarded by colleges and universities. Qualifies the holder to teach at the university level. Requires (usually published) research in the field. Typically requires an additional three to five years of study after earning a bachelor's degree. Anyone with a doctorate degree is addressed as a "doctor," not just medical doctors.

e-mail marketing: the process of sending a commercial message, typically to a group of people, using e-mail. In the most general sense, every e-mail sent to a potential or current customer can be considered e-mail marketing. It involves the use of e-mail to send advertisements, request business, inform subscribers about news, or solicit sales or donations.

entrepreneur: a person who starts, organizes, and manages a business (often a new business) and is responsible for the financial risk involved.

fourth estate: a term used to define the media and their role in society.

freelancer: a person who owns his or her own business through which services are provided for a variety of clients.

gap year: a year between high school and college (or sometimes between college and postgraduate studies) whereby the student is not in school but is instead typically involved in volunteer programs (such as the Peace Corps), in travel experiences, or in work and teaching experiences.

general education development (GED) degree: a degree earned that is the equivalent to a high school diploma without graduating from a standard high school.

Google Analytics: a web analytics service offered by Google that tracks and reports website traffic. Web analytics professionals use this tool to collect data about their website visitors, such as how many people come to the site, how long they stay, which pages they visit, which areas they click on, and so on. The purpose is to analyze these data in order to improve a website, sell more product, or determine return on investment from advertising and other marketing efforts. Other options include Adobe Web Analytics, Watson Customer Experience Analytics by IBM, Mixpanel, and Webtrends Analytics.

grants: money to pay for postsecondary education that is typically awarded to students who have financial need but can also be used in the areas of athletics, academics, demographics, veteran support, and special talents. Grants do not have to be paid back.

HTML: stands for Hypertext Markup Language. It's a simple markup language used to control how web pages look in a browser on the web. It can be enhanced by using Cascading Style Sheets and scripting languages, such as JavaScript.

master's degree: a secondary degree awarded by colleges and universities that requires at least one additional year of study after obtaining a bachelor's degree. The degree holder shows mastery of a specific field. Teachers in public school settings are often required to pursue their master's degrees after having worked as a teacher for a prescribed amount of time.

multimedia art: artwork created with new media technologies and computers.

online portfolio: an organized presentation of creative work on a website, blog, or social media site.

paid search/pay-per-click (PPC): an Internet advertising model used to encourage traffic to websites in which the advertiser pays a publisher (of the web page) when the ad is clicked. Pay-per-click is commonly associated with first-tier search engines. Search returns with the word "ad" at the top are examples of PPCs.

personal statement: a written description of your accomplishments, outlook, interests, goals, and personality that's an important part of your college application. The personal statement should set you apart from others. The required length depends on the institution, but they generally range from one to two pages, or 500 to 1,000 words.

Photoshop: Adobe's illustration and design tool that allows you to create and edit computer graphics images that are in the raster graphics format (essentially, JPEG, PING, or GIF). Most of its features are built for editing and retouching digital photographs. However, Photoshop can also edit digital video frames, render text, create 3D modeling features, and develop design elements contents for websites. Like most of Adobe's products, it's geared toward professional design and multimedia development.

podcast: a spoken-word digital audio file made available on the internet for downloading to a computer or mobile device.[1] They are typically available as episodic series, new installments of which are received by subscribers automatically. Streaming applications and podcasting services provide a convenient and integrated way to manage podcast consumption. *See also* podcast producers.

podcast producers: professionals who publish podcasts for audio consumption. They often develop shows and episode content, write scripts and stories, and help find and hire guests to speak on the podcast, for example. They are also typically involved in the audio recording and editing processes. *See also* podcast.

portfolio: work selected by a creative person to share with potential clients or associates that best represents their style and current work.

postsecondary degree: an educational degree above and beyond a high school education. This is a general description that includes trade certificates and certifications, associate degrees, bachelor's degrees, master's degrees, and beyond.

scholarships: merit-based aid used to pay for postsecondary education that does not have to be paid back. Scholarships are typically awarded on the basis of academic excellence or some other special talent, such as music or art.

Scholastic Aptitude Test (SAT): one of the standardized tests in the United States that anyone applying to undergraduate studies should take. It measures verbal and mathematical reasoning abilities as they relate to predicting successful performance in college. It is intended to complement a student's grade-point average and school record in assessing readiness for college. The total score of the SAT is 1,600. *See also* American College Test.

search engine optimization (SEO): the practice of improving the visitor traffic (the quality and quantity of visitors) to your website or web page from search engines.[2] SEO is specifically through nonpaid (also known as "organic") search engine results. *See also* paid search/pay-per-click; web analytics specialists.

social media specialists: workers who plan, implement, and monitor a company's social media strategy and online reputation in order to increase brand awareness, improve the company's marketing efforts, and increase overall sales. They create and administer content on all social media platforms, such as Facebook, Instagram, and Twitter, to build an audience and encourage customer engagement.

user experience (UX) design: a design process that focuses on creating a user experience that is favorable and even leads users to certain conclusions, such as a buying point. By creating user interactions that are pleasant and desirable, the design becomes meaningful and relevant to the users. UX design usually considers aspects of branding, design, usability, and function.

user interface design: the visual layout of the actual elements (such as buttons, icons, lists, and graphics) that users can interact with at a website or technological product. Often refers to the visual layout of a web page or smartphone screen.

web analytics specialists: workers who determine the costs, benefits, and effectiveness of websites by gathering and interpreting the traffic to the site (such as how many visitors come to the site, which pages they visit, which areas they click on, how long they stay, and so on). *See also* Google Analytics.

web app: an application that runs in a web browser. A common example is a web-mail application like Gmail, which stores your account data (your e-mail) in the Google cloud. You can access a web application from any computer connected to the internet using a standard browser. Web apps are typically platform/operating system independent since the website serves as the user interface.

web development: a broad term that refers to the varied tasks involved in creating a website or web application that will be hosted on the internet or on a local intranet. Web development includes designing the interface and the website; creating, programming, testing, and formatting the web content; client-side/server-side scripting for handling user interactions; managing and configuring network security; and more.

wireframe layout: a visual guide that shows the skeletal framework of a design piece, such as a website. They are created to help visualize and arrange elements for best results before the details are added. For websites, wireframes usually show which elements will exist on which pages. Different from a mock-up, which usually shows more visual details (such as colors, type used, and other elements).

Further Resources

Are you looking for more information about the fields within the "digital communications" umbrella, which in this book includes content creation specialists, podcast producers, digital advertising and marketing specialists, and social media managers? Or do you want to know more about the application process or need some help finding the right educational/vocational fit for you? Try these resources as a starting point on your journey toward finding a great career!

Books

Dover, Danny, and Erik Dafforn. *Search Engine Optimization Secrets*. Hoboken, NJ: Wiley 2011.

Fiske, Edward. *Fiske Guide to Colleges*. Naperville, IL: Sourcebooks, 2018.

Muchnick, Justin Ross. *Teens' Guide to College and Career Planning*. 12th ed. Lawrenceville, NJ: Peterson's Publishing, 2015.

Princeton Review. *The Best 382 Colleges, 2018 Edition: Everything You Need to Make the Right College Choice*. New York: Princeton Review, 2018.

Websites

American Gap Year Association

www.gapyearassociation.org

The American Gap Year Association's mission is "making transformative gap years an accessible option for all high school graduates." A gap year is a year taken between high school and college to travel, teach, work, volunteer, generally mature, and otherwise experience the world. Their website has lots of advice and resources for anyone considering taking a gap year.

American Indian College Fund
https://collegefund.org
Provides scholarships and college information for Native American students at any of the nation's 33 accredited tribal colleges and universities.

The Balance Website
www.thebalance.com
This site is all about managing money and finances but also has a large section called "Your Career," which provides advice for writing résumés and cover letters, interviewing, and more. Search the site for teens and you can find teen-specific advice and tips.

Cappex
www.cappex.com
A free website where you can find out about colleges and merit aid scholarships.

College Board Website
www.collegeboard.org
The College Entrance Examination Board tracks and summarizes financial data from colleges and universities all over the United States. This site can be your one-stop shop for all things college research. It contains lots of advice and information about taking and doing well on the SAT and ACT tests, many articles on college planning, a robust college search feature, a scholarship search feature, and a major and career search area. You can type your career of interest (e.g., digital advertising) into the search box and get back a full page that describes the career and gives advice on how to prepare, where to get experience, how to pay for it, and what characteristics you should have to excel in this career. It also contains lists of helpful classes to take while in high school and lots of links for more information. A great, well-organized site.

College Grad Career Profile Website
www.collegegrad.com/careers
Although this site is geared primarily to college graduates, the careers profile area has a list of links to nearly every career you could ever think of. A single click takes you to a detailed, helpful section that describes the job in detail, explains the educational requirements, includes links to good colleges that

offer this career, includes links to actual open jobs and internships, describes the licensing requirements (if any), lists salaries, and much more.

Gates Millennium Scholars

https://gmsp.org

Provides scholarships to reduce barriers to college for African American, American Indian/Alaska Native, Asian Pacific Islander American, and Hispanic American students regardless of major.

GoCollege

www.gocollege.com

Calls itself the number one college-bound website on the internet. Includes lots of good tips and information about getting money and scholarships for college and getting the most out of your college education. Has a good section on how scholarships in general work.

Go Overseas

www.gooverseas.com

Claims to be your guide to more than 14,000 study and teach abroad programs that will change how you see the world. Also includes information about high school abroad programs, and gap-year opportunities. Includes community reviews and information about finding programs specific to your interests and grade-level teaching aspirations.

Kahn Academy

www.khanacademy.org

An impressive collection of articles, courses, and videos about many educational topics in math, science, and the humanities. You can search any topic or subject (by subject matter and grade) and read lessons, take courses, and watch videos to learn all about it. Includes test prep information for the SAT, ACT, AP, GMAT, and other standardized tests. There is also a "College Admissions" tab with lots of good articles and information provided in the approachable Kahn style.

Live Career Website

www.livecareer.com

This site has an impressive number of resources directed to teens for writing résumés, cover letters, and interviewing.

Mapping Your Future

www.mappingyourfuture.org

This site helps young people figure out what they want to do and maps out how to reach career goals. Includes helpful tips on résumé writing, job hunting, job interviewing, and more.

Monster

www.monster.com

Perhaps the most well-known and certainly one of the largest employment websites in the United States. You fill in a couple of search boxes, and away you go. You can sort by job title, of course, as well as by company name, location, salary range, experience range, and much more. The site also includes information about career fairs, advice on résumés and interviewing, and more.

Peterson's College Prep Website

www.petersons.com

In addition to lots of information about preparing for the ACT and SAT tests and easily searchable information about scholarships nationwide, Peterson's site includes a comprehensive search feature to for universities and schools based on location, major, name, and more.

Study.Com Website

www.study.com

A site similar to Kahn Academy where you can search any topic or subject and read lessons, take courses, and watch videos to learn all about it. Includes a good collection of information about the digital communications professions.

TeenLife: College Preparation

www.teenlife.com

This organization calls itself "the leading source for college preparation," and it includes lots of information about summer programs, gap-year programs, community service, and more. They believe that spending time out "in the world" outside of the classroom can help students develop important life skills. This site contains lots of links to volunteer and summer programs.

U.S. Bureau of Labor Statistics

www.bls.gov

The U.S. Bureau of Labor Statistics produces this website. It offers lots of relevant and updated information about various careers, including average salaries, how to work in the industry, the job's outlook in the job market, typical work environments, and what workers do on the job. See www.bls.gov/emp for a full list of employment projections.

U.S. News & World Report **College Rankings**

www.usnews.com/best-colleges

U.S. News & World Report provides almost 50 different types of numerical rankings and lists of colleges throughout the United States to help students with their college search. You can search colleges by best reviewed, best value for the money, best liberal arts schools, best schools for B students, and more.

Bibliography

"Active Listening: Hear What People Are Really Saying." *Mind Tools*. Accessed November 29, 2020, www.mindtools.com/CommSkll/ActiveListening.htm.

Adler, Lou. "New Survey Reveals 85 Percent of All Jobs Are Filled via Networking." *LinkedIn.com*, February 29, 2016. Accessed November 29, 2020, www.linkedin.com/pulse/new-survey-reveals-85-all-jobs-filled-via-net working-lou-adler.

Asimov, Isaac. *The Roving Mind*. Amherst, NY: Prometheus Books, 1983.

Boyle, Justin. "How Much Does Trade School Cost?" *Real Work Matters*, September 21, 2019. Accessed November 14, 2020, www.rwm.org/articles /how-much-does-trade-school-cost.

"Career Choices." *Balance.com*, April 24, 2018. Accessed November 12, 2020, www.thebalance.com/career-choice-or-change-4161891.

Common Core State Standards Initiative. "Preparing American's Students for Success." Accessed October 20, 2020, www.corestandards.org.

Fiske, Edward. *Fiske Guide to Colleges*. Naperville, IL: Sourcebooks, 2018.

Gap Year Association. "Gap Year Data and Benefits." Accessed September 12, 2020, www.gapyearassociation.org/data-benefits.php.

"Healthcare Occupations." Various tabs. *Bureau of Labor Statistics, U.S. Department of Labor*, updated April 9, 2021. Accessed November 12, 2020, www.bls.gov/ooh/healthcare.

Keates, Cathy. "What Is Job Shadowing?" *TalentEgg*. Accessed November 9, 2020, https://talentegg.ca/incubator/2011/02/03/what-is-job-shadowing.

"Keeping an Eye on Recruiter Behavior." *Ladders*, 2018. Accessed October 20, 2020, https://cdn.theladders.net/static/images/basicSite/pdfs/TheLadders-EyeTracking-StudyC2.pdf.

"Learn What's New with the FAFSA Process." *U.S. Department of Education*. Accessed December 14, 2020, https://financialaidtoolkit.ed.gov/tk/learn /fafsa/updates.jsp.

Muchnick, Justin Ross. *Teens' Guide to College and Career Planning.* 12th ed. Lawrenceville, NJ: Peterson's Publishing, 2015.

National Center for Education Statistics. "Fast Facts: Graduation Rates." Updated January 2018. Accessed September 19, 2020, https://nces.ed.gov /fastfacts/display.asp?id=40.

———. "Private School Enrollment." Updated January 2018. Accessed November 29, 2020, https://nces.ed.gov/programs/coe/indicator_cgc.asp.

"Press Releases." *CareerBuilder.com.* Accessed November 29, 2020, www .careerbuilder.com/share/aboutus/pressreleasesdetail.aspx?ed=12%2F31 %2F2016&id=pr945&sd=4%2F28%2F2016.

Ryan, Liz. "Twelve Qualities Employers Look for When They're Hiring." *Forbes.com,* May 2, 2016. Accessed October 10, 2020, www.forbes.com /sites/lizryan/2016/03/02/12-qualities-employers-look-for-when-they re-hiring/#8ba06d22c242.

"Types of Scholarships." *Go College.* Accessed September 30, 2020, www.go college.com/financial-aid/scholarships/types.

"Understanding College Costs." *College Entrance Examination Board.* Accessed November 24, 2020, https://bigfuture.collegeboard.org/pay-for-college /college-costs/understanding-college-costs.

U.S. Department of Education. "Focusing Higher Education on Student Success." July 27, 2015. Accessed November 30, 2020, www.ed.gov/news /press-releases/fact-sheet-focusing-higher-education-student-success.

Van Buskirk, Peter. "Finding a Good College Fit." *U.S. News & World Report,* June 13, 2011. Accessed November 30, 2020, www.usnews.com /education/blogs/the-college-admissions-insider/2011/06/13/finding -a-good-college-fit.

Waldman, Joshua. *Job Searching with Social Media for Dummies.* 2nd ed. Hoboken, NJ: Wiley, 2013.

About the Author

Kezia Endsley is an editor and author from Indianapolis, Indiana. In addition to editing technical publications and writing books for teens, she enjoys running and triathlons, traveling, reading, and spending time with her family and many pets.